The French Resistance Against Nazi Occupation

The French Resistance Against Nazi Occupation

A Model For Palestinian Resistance

GEW Reports and Analyses Team

Hichem Karoui (Editor)

Global East-West For Studies and Publishing

CONTENTS ▊

CONTENTS

EPIGRAPHS

"Whatever happens, the flame of the French resistance must not and shall not die." **Charles de Gaulle's Appeal of 18 June.**

"Freedom is what you do with what's been done to you." **Jean-Paul Sartre, "Paris Under the Occupation".**

"I carry within me the plagues of all those who fight for freedom." **Albert Camus, "The Blood of Freedom".**

"Tyranny has not triumphed; the enemy who is trying to conquer us from the outside has not succeeded in robbing us of our intimate alliance with the universe." **Antoine de Saint-Exupéry, "Letter to a Hostage".**

"Nicole Minet", a French Partisan who
captured 25 Nazis in the Chartres area
(August 1944: public domain).

ABOUT THIS COLLECTION

In this compelling and thought-provoking collection of books labelled "Resistances," produced by GEW Reports & Analyses, we embark on an immersive voyage through the rich tapestry of history, unveiling the heroic narratives of movements that steadfastly resisted the waves of oppression, colonisation, and exploitation. Beyond being a mere historical account, this collection is a tribute to the unbreakable spirit of resistance reverberating across the globe — from the bustling streets of North Africa and the Middle East to the far corners where Buddhist and Marxist ideologies intertwined with the quest for emancipation.

Each volume within this collection is a dedicated exploration of a distinct nation: Tunisia, Algeria, Morocco, Egypt, Sudan, Syria, Iraq, Lebanon, but also the USA (civil rights struggle), China (100 years of humiliation), South Africa (Apartheid), Vietnam, Indochina, India, among others, delving deeply into their distinctive struggles against a shared antagonist — the imperialist West. The narrative transcends conflicts; it offers an illuminating journey into how ideologies such as Islam, Marxism, and Buddhism have acted as catalysts and guiding philosophies for these remarkable movements.

This collection's heart lies in the enduring struggle in Palestine, set against a broader historical and geopolitical canvas backdrop. The Palestinian resistance against Israeli occupation, depicted here as an extension of Western imperialism, is presented with profound insight and perspective, challenging conventional narratives. This collection fearlessly confronts the dissonance between the West's professed ideals of democracy and human rights and its actions, often at odds with these principles.

"Resistances" serves a dual purpose. Firstly, it serves as an educational beacon, enlightening younger generations about the often unspoken stories of people living under the yoke of colonisation and their relentless pursuit of freedom. Secondly, it seeks to shed light on the injustices perpetrated by Western powers, offering a critical examination of their support for expansionist and oppressive policies while categorising those who resist as 'terrorists', despite international law recognising the right to resist occupation.

Is Hamas and other Palestinian organisations that resist the military occupation "terrorist" organisations? No, they are not. The United Nations General Assembly (UNGA) has explicitly affirmed the right of Palestinians to resist Israel's military occupation, *including through armed struggle*. This right was affirmed in the context of the right to self-determination of all peoples under foreign and colonial rule. Some of the most relevant UN resolutions on this matter include:

- UNGA Resolution 3314 (1974) affirmed the right of self-determination, freedom, and independence for all "peoples under colonial and racist regimes or other forms of alien domination." It affirmed the "right of these peoples to struggle to that end and to seek and receive support."[1]
- UNGA Resolution 37/43 (1982) reaffirmed the "inalienable right" of the Palestinian people "and all peoples under foreign and colonial domination" to self-determination. It also reiterates the legitimacy of "the struggle of peoples for [...] liberation from colonial and foreign domination and foreign occupation by all available means, including armed struggle."[2]

Similar principles have been repeated in numerous other UNGA resolutions. Although UNGA resolutions are not legally binding, they "accurately reflect the customary international legal opinion among the majority of the world's sovereign states."[3]

In international law, the right to resist is closely related to the principle of self-determination. It is widely recognised that a right to self-determination arises in situations of colonial domination, foreign occupation, and racist regimes that deny a segment of the population political participation. All this applies to the Israeli occupation of Palestine.

For instance, international law legitimises Palestinian attempts to resist Israeli oppression[4]. The International Bill of Human Rights also implicitly teaches the right to resist oppression. The preamble to the Universal Declaration of Human Rights states that it is essential for human rights to be protected by the rule of law to prevent individuals from resorting to rebellion against tyranny and oppression[5].

Anti-colonial movements, a form of resistance against colonial rule, have been instrumental in the struggle for self-determination in colonised countries (Tunisia, Algeria, Egypt, Sudan, China, Vietnam, etc.) These movements have often been concerned with the world that decolonised nations were to inherit collectively[6].

The right to resist oppression and colonisation is a fundamental human right recognised in international law and human rights instruments. Nothing could change this fact, even if the USA and Europe, still clinging to their old imperialist traditions, stand alone on the planet against the Right to Resist until the end of times.

This collection is a testament to the indomitable human spirit and the unwavering quest for freedom and justice. It is a scholarly opus, meticulously researched and presented. Yet, it is also a narrative that speaks to the soul, serving as a reminder of the universal values of liberty and dignity. As the editor and publisher, I am honoured to introduce this "Resistances" collection, firmly believing that it will inspire our readers, encouraging them to view history and contemporary events through a lens of nuanced comprehension and empathy.

We extend a warm invitation to embark on this extraordinary journey through "Resistances," where you will uncover the hitherto untold tales of courage, resilience, and the relentless pursuit of justice that have profoundly shaped our world.

Hichem Karoui

Senior Researcher and Editor of the "Resistances" collection.

London, 24 November 2023

References

1.   UNGA resolution 3314, "Definition of Aggression," December 14, 1974.

2.   UNGA resolution 37/43, "Importance of the universal realization of the right of peoples to self-determination and of the speedy granting of independence to colonial countries and peoples for the effective guarantee and observance of human rights," December 3, 1982.

3.   John Sigler, "Palestine: Legitimate Armed Resistance vs. Terrorism," *Electronic Intifada,* May 17 2004.

4.   Werleman, Cj. "International Law Guarantees Palestinians the Right to Resist." International law guarantees Palestinians the right to resist, May 28, 2018. https://www.trtworld.com/opinion/international-law-guarantees-palestinians-the-right-to-resist-17810.

5.   United Nations. "Universal Declaration of Human Rights | United Nations," n.d. https://www.un.org/en/about-us/universal-declaration-of-human-rights.

6.   Elam, J. Daniel. Global South Studies, U.Va. "Anti-colonialism," n.d. https://globalsouthstudies.as.virginia.edu/key-concepts/anticolonialism.

To the valiant Palestinians who are resisting the imposition of a fascist Zionist entity by fascist imperialist powers.
Freedom is a human right, as is the freedom to oppose injustice and oppression in whatever way.
They can't keep the truth hidden forever when it's shining like the sun over our heads and enlightening the planet.

The French Model of Resistance
Inspires Palestinians

Although many people in France and the West, blinded by pro-Zionist intoxicating propaganda, consider "Hamas" (an Arabic acronym for the Palestinian Islamic Resistance Movement) a terrorist organisation, the truth is that Hamas and other national resistance movements, including the French during the Nazi occupation, were also labelled "terrorists" by their enemies. While the present book is not concerned with the Palestinian issue, it will show the readers that the French resistance struggling against an invading power did precisely what some French political leaders are blaming the Palestinian nationalists for, overlooking the fact that there are no differences between the resistance movements which always make the same choice of armed struggle until liberation.

The French Resistance Against Nazi Occupation: A Model for Global Liberation Movements

The French Resistance against Nazi Occupation is a remarkable testament to the courage, resilience, and unyielding spirit of human determination in the face of overwhelming adversity. As we begin our journey through Volume 2 of "Resistances," we delve into the narrative of an era that not only shaped the fate of a nation but also echoed across continents, inspiring other liberation movements, including the Palestinian Resistance against Israeli occupation, regardless of political leanings (i.e. Hamas and Islamic Jihad included). It is important to remember that the French Resistance against the Nazis, led by General de Gaulle, did not exclude the French communists and socialists, who were an essential part of the network's core. Some of the greatest French intellectuals, such as Aragon, R. Char, Eluard, Prevert, Sartre, de Beauvoir, Malraux, Camus and many others, have celebrated this fact. In other words, no one was labelled as "extremist," and no ideology was deemed unfit for the cause, as there is nothing more important than unity in the face of a common enemy occupying the country.

Importance of the French Resistance

In the annals of history, the French Resistance occupies a pivotal place, symbolising the collective will of a nation to resist oppression, uphold freedom, and protect the very essence of human dignity. It provides a compelling account of individual heroism and collective endeavour in pursuing liberty and justice.

Roots of the French Resistance

Before the harrowing days of Nazi Occupation, France revelled in its cultural richness, intellectual fervour, and vibrant spirit, an essence that would form the bedrock of future resistance. However, the rapid and imposing ascendancy of Nazi forces eclipsed this vibrancy, casting a shadow of fear and oppression over the nation.

Key Figures and Movements

At the heart of the Resistance stood Charles de Gaulle, whose unwavering commitment and vision coalesced into the formation of Free France, serving as the torchbearer of hope and unity for those yearning for liberation. Alongside de Gaulle's leadership, the emergence of Maquis and various guerrilla movements further fuelled the flames of resistance, striking at the very foundations of the occupation.

Underground Networks and Operations

Espionage, covert communication, and acts of sabotage became the arsenal of the French Resistance, driving forth a relentless campaign against the occupiers. Their clandestine activities disrupted the enemy and sowed the seeds of camaraderie and unwavering determination among the public.

Impact and Influence

The impact of the French Resistance transcended geographical boundaries, serving as a blueprint for other occupied nations and liberation movements worldwide. Its indelible imprint on the international stage became a source of inspiration and a testament to the power of unity and defiance, most and foremost for the countries France has occupied since the XIXth century: Tunisia, Algeria, Morrocco, etc...

Comparison to Other Movements

The resonance of the French Resistance echoes within the struggle of countless other liberation movements, notably the Palestinian Resistance against Israeli occupation, drawing parallels in the pursuit of sovereignty, self-determination, and the unyielding spirit against oppressive forces.

Challenges and Sacrifices

The path of resistance was fraught with peril, and those who dared to defy the occupation faced unspeakable risks, enduring the dual agony of personal sacrifice and witnessing the suffering of their compatriots. The everyday life under occupation was a testament to their unbroken spirit, courage, and resilience.

Women in the Resistance

French women played an indomitable role in the Resistance, much like the Palestinian women today, defying societal norms and contributing significantly to the cause. Their invaluable contributions and sacrifices too often went unnoticed, and yet they stood as pillars of strength and determination, shaping the course of history.

Intellectual and Cultural Resistance

In a poignant display of defiance, the Resistance relied on literature, art, and underground press to keep the flame of hope alive. They defied the oppressors through intellectual and cultural expression, inspiring the masses to stand firm against tyranny.

Allies and Collaboration

Strategic collaboration with Allied forces and coordination with other resistance movements secured the French Resistance's position as a pivotal force against tyranny while also highlighting the power of solidarity and unity in the face of a common foe.

Post-War Ramifications

The aftermath of the war brought forth a landscape marked by profound changes, as the nation began the arduous journey of reintegration, reconstruction, and the reshaping of its political and societal fabric, paving the way for enduring transformations.

Controversies and Reconciliation

The post-war era was also fraught with moral ambiguity and deep-seated controversies, demanding a reckoning with the past and the confronting of collaboration, an arduous yet necessary process in the pursuit of enduring justice and reconciliation.

Celebrating the Legacy

Through memorials, commemorations, and the preservation of stories, the legacy of the Resistance lives on, serving as a poignant reminder of the unyielding spirit and the indomitable will of those who stood against oppression.

Future Perception and Understanding

While the pages of history have turned, the lessons of the French Resistance remain pertinent, serving as a beacon of education and awareness, offering timeless insights for a world grappling with its challenges and oppressions.

Hichem Karoui

Introduction: France Under Nazi Occupation

The arrival of Nazi forces in France during World War II marked a dark and tumultuous time in the nation's history. From 1940 to 1944, the French people endured the hardships and oppressive rule imposed by the German occupation. This period tested the resilience, courage, and moral fortitude of individuals and communities who found themselves caught in the grip of a brutal regime.

The fall of France in 1940 was a devastating blow, as German forces swiftly overwhelmed French defences. The government, led by Marshal Philippe Pétain, signed an armistice with Germany, effectively surrendering control over large parts of France. With the establishment of the Vichy regime, which collaborated with the occupying forces, the country was divided into two distinct zones: the occupied zone, directly under German control, and the unoccupied zone, where the Vichy government held nominal authority.

Life under Nazi occupation was marked by fear and uncertainty. The Germans implemented a range of strict controls, suppressing free speech, imposing curfews, and instituting a system of surveillance that permeated all aspects of daily life. French citizens lived under constant scrutiny, with the Gestapo and its collaborators relentlessly hunting down suspected members of the Resistance.

Any act of defiance or resistance carried with it the risk of brutal reprisals. The occupying forces often responded to resistance activities with mass executions, reprisal killings, and widespread acts of terror to strike fear into the hearts of the French population. The infamous massacre at Oradour-sur-Glane, where an entire village was destroyed, and 642 civilians were murdered in reprisal for Resistance activities, stands as a chilling example of the occupier's brutality. A culture of fear and intimidation prevailed, making it all the more remarkable that individuals chose to stand up against the occupiers despite the grave risks involved.

Economic hardship and scarcity further compounded the challenges faced by the French people. German authorities diverted resources to support their war effort, leaving the French population to contend with food shortages and rationing. Basic necessities became luxuries, and the struggle for survival became a daily reality for many. The black market thrived as people sought to obtain essential goods through illicit means, while others relied on the generosity of individuals who risked their own safety to provide support.

Furthermore, the forced conscription of French workers into German industries left families torn apart and added to the burden of those remaining at home. The so-called "STO" (Service du Travail Obligatoire) forced approximately 600,000 young Frenchmen to work in German factories or on the Eastern Front. These individuals faced harsh conditions, often enduring brutal treatment and exploitation. The separation from their families compounded their anguish and propelled some to seek solace in acts of resistance.

However, amidst this bleak landscape, a spirit of resistance began to emerge. From the earliest days of the occupation, individuals and groups formed clandestine networks with the goal of undermining the Nazi regime and working towards the liberation of France. These networks, known collectively as the French Resistance, engaged in acts of sabotage, intelligence gathering, and disseminating clandestine information.

The Resistance was a diverse and decentralised movement, united by a shared determination to fight back against the occupiers. It consisted of individuals from various political backgrounds, social classes, and regions of France. Some were motivated by a deep sense of patriotism and the desire to regain French sovereignty, while others joined as a reaction to the oppressive measures imposed by the occupiers. Within the Resistance, multiple ideological factions coexisted, with communist, socialist, and liberal groups collaborating on common objectives despite their differing long-term visions for post-war France.

Life in the Resistance was perilous and demanding, requiring immense courage and an unwavering commitment to the cause. Operating in the shadows, the Resistance adapted and improvised to overcome the challenges posed by the German authorities. They established secret communication channels, utilising codes and ciphers to relay vital information without detection. Underground press and clandestine radio stations were set up to counter Nazi propaganda and to provide the French population with alternative sources of news and hope.

Acts of sabotage were carried out to disrupt German supply lines, hinder military operations, and erode the occupiers' control. Bridges and railways were sabotaged, military installations were targeted, and key personnel were assassinated. These acts not only inflicted material damage on the occupiers but also served as powerful symbols of defiance, showing that the occupation would not go unchallenged.

The Resistance was not without its internal debates, challenges, and dilemmas. The diverse nature of the movement led to differing strategies and aspirations. Some favoured overt acts of resistance, such as armed uprisings, while others advocated for more subtle means, such as gathering intelligence and disseminating anti-Nazi propaganda. These differing viewpoints often led to tensions and conflicts within the movement, but the common goal of liberation united the Resistance in their fight against the Nazi occupiers.

While the Nazi occupation of France was characterised by repression and collaboration, it also revealed the remarkable strength and resilience of the French people. Countless acts of bravery and sacrifice occurred, as individuals risked their lives to save others, protect vulnerable groups, and maintain a sense of national identity. The contributions of women in the Resistance were particularly significant, as they played crucial roles as couriers, intelligence gatherers, and fighters. Their efforts challenged societal norms and demonstrated that the struggle for freedom knows no gender boundaries.

As time went on, the Resistance gained momentum and expanded its activities. It developed into a well-organised network of cells, each with its own specialised tasks and responsibilities. Some focused on gathering intelligence and transmitting it to the Allies, while others specialised in sabotage, helping to disrupt German military operations and hamper their war efforts. Aided by sympathetic French citizens who provided safe houses, resources, and information, the Resistance became an underground force to be reckoned with.

Despite their best efforts, the Resistance faced constant dangers and a pervasive sense of vulnerability. The Gestapo's relentless pursuit of Resistance members resulted in frequent arrests, torture, and imprisonment. Many Resistance fighters met a tragic end at the hands of their captors, their sacrifice becoming another testament to the profound lengths some were willing to go to resist oppression.

This book delves into the untold stories of the French Resistance, shining a light on the courageous individuals and their extraordinary efforts to resist and ultimately contribute to the liberation of France. By examining their struggles, the dilemmas they faced, and the impact they made, we gain a deeper understanding of the human spirit in the face of adversity and the enduring legacy of resistance for future generations. Through their sacrifices and acts of defiance, the men and women of the French Resistance fought to preserve their nation's honour and liberty and left an indelible mark on history.

Research and Further Reading References:

1. "Marianne in Chains: Daily Life in the Heart of France During the German Occupation" by Robert Gildea, published by Macmillan in 2002.

2. "Vichy France: Old Guard and New Order, 1940-1944" by Robert O. Paxton, originally published by Alfred A. Knopf in 1972.

3. "The Sorrow and the Pity" by Marcel Ophüls is a documentary film released in 1969. While not a book, it has had considerable scholarly impact as a source.

4. "Occupation: The Ordeal of France 1940-1944" by Ian Ousby, published by St. Martin's Press in 1997.

5. "Vichy France and the Jews" by Michael R. Marrus and Robert O. Paxton, originally published by Basic Books in 1981.

6. "Choices in Vichy France: The French Under Nazi Occupation" by John F. Sweets, published by Oxford University Press in 1986.

7. "Scientific Information in Occupied France, 1940-1944" by PS Richards, explores the impact of Nazi occupation on scientific research in France. https://www.jstor.org/stable/4308716

8. "Nazi Paris: The History of an Occupation, 1940-1944" provides an in-depth analysis of Nazi Germany's rule in France, with a focus on Paris as the centre of occupation. https://www.jstor.org/stable/j.ctt9qcvnx

III

The Seeds of Resistance: Pre-War Conditions and Movements

To fully comprehend the roots of the French Resistance movement during World War II, it is crucial to examine the pre-war circumstances and political movements that established the foundation for opposition to Nazi occupation. France, alongside numerous other nations during that time, was characterized by political instability, economic challenges, and social turmoil, all of which would play a role in developing resistance networks.

Throughout the 1930s, France faced many challenges that deeply impacted its society and fuelled dissatisfaction with the government. The Great Depression severely impacted the country, resulting in high unemployment and widespread poverty. As economic disparities widened, so did political divisions. The rise of fascist and far-right movements, such as the Croix de Feu and the Action Française, presented an alarming threat to democratic values and peace.

The Croix de Feu, founded by Colonel François de la Rocque, captured the attention of disillusioned World War I veterans and conservative elements of French society. Its members espoused a nationalist ideology, emphasising traditional values and advocating for a strong central government. The Action Française, led by Charles Maurras, propagated an extreme form of nationalism that glorified the monarchy and emphasised the cultural superiority of the French nation.

Simultaneously, left-wing political movements gained momentum, aiming to address social and economic inequalities. The French Communist Party (PCF), in particular, experienced a surge in popularity and membership, drawing support from workers and intellectuals who sought radical change. The PCF positioned itself as the vanguard of the proletarian revolution and actively pushed for a united front against fascism. However, these political divisions also laid the groundwork for internal conflicts within the resistance movement later on, as rivalries between different factions often overshadowed the common goal of fighting Nazi occupation.

The Popular Front government, formed in 1936 and supported by a coalition of left-wing parties, introduced significant social reforms, such as the 40-hour workweek and paid vacations. These measures aimed to appease the working class and curb the appeal of extremist movements. However, their implementation faced significant opposition from conservative elements of society, who feared the growing influence of communism and socialism.

The Spanish Civil War (1936-1939) shaped the French resistance. The conflict served as a battleground for ideologies, with Republican forces supported by left-wing factions, while General Franco's Nationalists received backing from fascist states. Many French volunteers joined the International Brigades to fight against fascism in Spain, establishing connections and gaining invaluable experience that would prove crucial in the resistance against the Nazis.

Simultaneously, the Spanish Civil War aroused the interest and sympathy of French intellectuals and artists. They were deeply affected by the Republican cause, seeing it as a struggle against the forces of oppression and the rise of totalitarianism. Artists such as Pablo Picasso, Max Ernst, and André Malraux became politically engaged and used their talents to denounce fascism and raise awareness about the Spanish conflict. Their experiences in Spain, alongside their interactions with Spanish refugees fleeing to France, further fuelled their determination to resist the Nazi regime.

The outbreak of World War II in 1939 only further intensified the political landscape in France. The swift German invasion in 1940 resulted in the fall of France and the establishment of the Vichy regime, a collaborationist government under Marshal Philippe Pétain. While some French citizens accepted this new order, others quickly resisted.

Emerging from various pre-war political movements, including communist, socialist, and anarchist groups, the seeds of resistance sprouted in the face of shared outrage and determination to reclaim their freedoms. The remnants of the Republican forces from the Spanish Civil War and military officials who refused to surrender to Germany formed the core of resistance movements. They were quickly joined by intellectuals, students, trade unions, and ordinary citizens who refused to accept the occupation.

These early resistance networks operated clandestinely, organising secret meetings, distributing subversive literature, and spreading anti-Nazi propaganda. They aimed to maintain hope within a population devastated by defeat and lay the groundwork for future resistance actions. Intellectuals played a significant role in establishing connections between disparate groups and disseminating critical information. Renowned writer and philosopher Jean-Paul Sartre, for example, used his influential position and literary skills to denounce Vichy and Nazi policies, inspiring others to resist.

In addition to political motivations, personal convictions and a deep sense of patriotism played a significant role in fuelling resistance efforts. Many viewed the German occupation as a direct threat to French identity, culture, and sovereignty and were willing to risk their lives to protect their nation. Poetry and literature became resistance tools, offering expressions of defiance and unity. Works by renowned writers such as Paul Éluard, Louis Aragon, and Robert Desnos often contained coded messages that veiled acts of resistance, allowing their words to reach a wider audience while evading Nazi censorship.

As the pre-war conditions and movements set the stage for resistance, it became clear that the French people were not willing to accept Nazi domination without a fight. The seeds of resistance had been sown, nourished by the shared outrage and determination of a nation refusing to submit to tyranny. These early networks would lay the foundation for a powerful and resilient movement that would defy the Nazi regime and contribute to the eventual liberation of France.

The struggles and divisions within the pre-war political landscape continued to impact the development of the resistance movement. The French Communist Party, following the Molotov-Ribbentrop Pact between Nazi Germany and the Soviet Union, shifted its stance away from promoting immediate resistance. The party declared the war as "imperialist" rather than anti-fascist, leading to confusion and disillusionment among its members. This shift created tensions and divisions within the more significant resistance movement, as communist members struggled to reconcile the party's changing stance with their desire to fight against Nazi occupation.

Furthermore, Vichy France, under the leadership of Pétain, aimed at maintaining an appearance of French sovereignty while collaborating with Nazi Germany. Many in France, however, saw through the façade of the Vichy regime and recognised it as a puppet government serving the interests of the occupiers. The blatant collaboration by certain French officials further fuelled the determination to resist.

Resistance efforts were not limited to political and intellectual circles; trade unions also significantly mobilised resistance activities. The General Confederation of Labour (CGT), historically tied to the French Communist Party, coordinated strikes and acts of sabotage, disrupting the German war machine and hindering their efforts in France. Additionally, smaller trade union movements, such as the more anarchist-leaning National Confederation of Labour (CNT), pursued their agendas within the resistance.

Religious communities also made significant contributions to the resistance movement. Both Catholic and Protestant leaders denounced Nazi ideology and collaborated with resistance members. The Catholic Church, for example, actively participated in providing shelter and assistance to Jewish individuals targeted by the Nazis. Some Catholic priests and Protestant pastors even went as far as risking their lives to hide Jewish families and smuggle them to safety.

France's pre-war conditions and movements provided fertile ground for resistance to take root. The deep divisions, shaped by political ideologies and economic hardships, motivated individuals from various backgrounds to come together to fight against Nazi occupation. Whether driven by political convictions, personal beliefs, or a deep sense of patriotism, these individuals formed the early networks of resistance, using clandestine methods to organise and carry out acts of defiance against the Nazis and their collaborators.

The resistance movement faced immense challenges from the start. The German occupation forces were highly organised and merciless in suppressing any defiance. Nazi propaganda and surveillance made it difficult to operate covertly or communicate without risking arrest or execution. Additionally, the Vichy regime actively collaborated with the Nazis, using its police force to hunt down resistance members and suppress any acts of resistance.

However, despite these obstacles, the seeds of resistance persisted. Underground networks expanded and became more sophisticated, with members specialising in different areas such as intelligence gathering, sabotage, and organising escape routes for Allied soldiers and downed pilots. The resistance also established connections with the British Special Operations Executive (SOE), who provided training, weapons, and support to resistance fighters.

One of the most significant early acts of resistance was the creation of the National Council of the Resistance (CNR) in May 1943. The CNR united various resistance groups under a common goal: the liberation of France and the restoration of a democratic government. The CNR acted as a central coordinating body, led by figures such as Jean Moulin and Pierre Brossolette, facilitating communication and collaboration between different resistance networks. It also played a pivotal role in formulating a vision for post-war France, with its programme calling for social and economic reforms to address past injustices and build a more equitable society.

However, the resistance movement was not without its internal conflicts and tensions. As mentioned earlier, the division within the French Communist Party caused significant rifts within the broader resistance movement. These ideological differences often led to rivalries and compromises that hindered cooperation as various factions and groups jockeyed for influence and control.

Nevertheless, the resistance persisted and grew stronger as the war progressed. Acts of sabotage, intelligence gathering, and armed resistance became more frequent and daring. Resistance fighters provided vital assistance to the Allied forces during the D-Day invasion in June 1944, sabotaging German supply lines and disrupting communication networks. They also played a crucial role in supporting the advance of Allied troops after the liberation of Paris.

The sacrifices made by the resistance were immense. Thousands of fighters were captured, tortured, and executed by the Nazis. Countless others lost their lives in acts of sabotage, armed resistance, or as victims of Nazi reprisals. Resistance members who were captured and survived the war often faced the devastating consequences of their actions, with many enduring imprisonment or suffering lasting physical and psychological trauma.

The legacy of the resistance movement is a testament to the power of collective action and a refusal to accept oppression. It serves as a reminder of the resilience of the human spirit and the bravery of those who risked everything to protect their nation, democracy, and fellow citizens. The seeds of resistance, sown in the tumultuous pre-war conditions and movements, sprouted into a powerful and formidable force that played a vital role in the eventual liberation of France.

Research and Further Reading References:

Some of the key scholarly works that focus on the seeds of the French resistance and the pre-war conditions and movements in France include:

1. "The French Resistance" by Olivier Wieviorka, published by Harvard University Press in 2016 (original French edition in 2013), provides a comprehensive examination of the nature and origins of the Resistance in France.

2. "Fighters in the Shadows: A New History of the French Resistance" by Robert Gildea, published by Faber & Faber in 2015, offers a broad portrait of the disparate resistance movements.

3. "France and the Spanish Civil War: Cultural Representations of the War Next Door, 1936-1945" by Martin Hurcombe, published by Ashgate in 2011, discusses France's intellectual and political climate before World War II and the impact of the Spanish Civil War.

4. "French Communism in the Era of Stalin: The Quest for Unity and Integration, 1945-1962" by Irwin M. Wall, published by Greenwood Press in 1983, analyses the French Communist Party's position, which was crucial during the resistance and pre-war period.

5. "The Resistance: The French Fight Against the Nazis" by Matthew Cobb, published by Simon & Schuster in 2009. This work captures the contributions and struggles of those who fought against Nazi occupation.

These works provide a deep understanding of France's conditions, political landscape, and movements before and during World War II, which set the stage for the emergence of the Resistance. Some articles also are interesting for the researcher or the student who wants to go further:

1. "Nationalism, Collaboration, and Resistance: France under Nazi Occupation": This article explores nationalism, collaboration, and resistance during the German occupation

of France: https://direct.mit.edu/isec/article/43/2/117/12207/Nationalism-Collaboration-and-Resistance-France

2. "The Civilian Experience in German Occupied France, 1940...": This source includes a citation for "Some Sources on the Resistance Movement in France during the Nazi Occupation," published in The Journal of Modern History in 1946: https://digitalcommons.conncoll.edu/cgi/viewcontent.cgi?article=1005&context=histhp

4. "Some Sources on the Resistance Movement in France...": This article, written by FL Hadsel in 1946, mentions the files of the German armistice as important documents on conditions in France during the Nazi occupation: https://www.jstor.org/stable/1876308

IV

The Call to Arms: Formation of French Resistance Networks

In the darkest hours of France's occupation by Nazi forces, a call to arms resonated throughout the country. The French people, yearning for liberation and freedom, answered this call by forming various resistance networks to fight against the oppressors.

The formation of these networks was no easy task. The Nazi occupation had infiltrated every aspect of French society, stifling any form of dissent. However, courageous individuals from all walks of life faced the formidable challenge of organising resistance efforts.

One of the key factors that facilitated the formation of resistance networks was the pre-existing underground movements that had already been active before the occupation. These movements, including political parties, labour unions, and student groups, had long advocated for social justice and fighting against Fascism. Many members of these organisations quickly recognised the urgent need to resist the Nazis and adapted their existing structures and networks to serve the cause of liberation.

Within the French Communist Party (PCF) existed a clandestine organisation known as the Francs-Tireurs aet Partisans (FTP). While the PCF initially hesitated to engage in armed resistance openly, the FTP played a significant role in organising acts of sabotage and serving as a powerful underground force. Their members, operating covertly under the cover of guerrilla warfare, targeted German military installations, rail lines, and communication networks, effectively disrupting enemy operations.

Similarly, the socialist movement in France also contributed to the resistance efforts. The organisation known as Libération-Sud, born out of the newly formed Combat Zone, sought to combat the Fascist occupation through military means. Led by Emmanuel d'Astier dae La Vigerie, Libération-Sud engaged in acts of sabotage, disseminated anti-German propaganda, and supported the escape of political prisoners. With a strong emphasis on secrecy and security, Libération-Sud became one of France's most prominent resistance networks.

Another significant network that emerged during this time was the Front National (FN), also known as the National Front. The FN, led by leaders including Colonel Rémy, sought to unify various resistance organisations under a single umbrella, fostering cooperation and cohesion in the face of a common enemy. Their aims encompassed military resistance and political action, seeking to lay the groundwork for a free and democratic France once liberation was achieved.

Max Hymans, a former politician and civil servant, played a vital role in forming the Alliance network. The Alliance network connected multiple resistance groups and emphasised the importance of intelligence gathering and analysis. Their information and reports paved the way for strategic decision-making, enabling the resistance to stay one step ahead of the enemy.

The intelligence networks established by the resistance were crucial to their success. In addition to gathering information on German troop movements and activities, these networks also served as channels for disseminating instructions, coordinating actions, and identifying potential collaborators. Intelligence-gathering was a high-risk operation, requiring skilled operatives who could blend into their surroundings and elude detection. Espionage became a dangerous game of cat and mouse, with resistance members risking their lives to obtain vital information that could save countless others.

The formation of resistance networks involved extensive coordination, often occurring in secret and under constant threat of discovery. Cells were established, comprising a group of individuals who collaborated to carry out covert operations. These cells were designed to minimise risk by compartmentalising knowledge and reducing the potential impact of any single member's capture or betrayal. The individuals within the cells were often known only to a trusted few, protecting the network against infiltration.

Intricate codes and ciphers were developed to ensure effective communication between the various cells and resistance networks. These encryption methods allowed members to communicate discreetly, sharing vital information without fear of interception by the Nazis. Some resistance members mastered the art of creating their codes or working with existing codes, using everything from everyday objects to literary works as inspiration for their secret communication.

Additionally, liaisons were established between different networks to facilitate the sharing of intelligence and resources. These liaisons played a crucial role in passing information and building trust between various resistance groups. Different networks grew interconnected by establishing personal connections and sharing risks, developing a broader and more formidable resistance force.

The call to arms extended beyond traditional boundaries, bringing together people from diverse backgrounds. Intellectuals, artists, peasants, workers, and even clergy joined forces to fight against the occupation. Women played a crucial role, too, defying gender norms and contributing in various capacities, including intelligence gathering, sabotage, and nursing wounded resistance fighters. Women such as Simone Segouin (Nicole Minet), whose youthful audacity saw her fighting in many successful campaigns, became inspiring symbols of female resistance.

The resistance networks faced constant threats from Nazi collaborators and infiltrators. The Milice, a paramilitary organisation established by the Vichy regime, actively collaborated with the Nazis and targeted members of the resistance. Through acts of terrorism, intimidation, and ruthless interrogations, they sought to dismantle and destroy the resistance networks. Resistance fighters faced the constant danger of arrest, torture, and deportation to concentration camps.

As the resistance networks grew stronger and more organised, they began carrying out acts of sabotage against the German war machine. Railways were sabotaged, munitions factories targeted, and communication lines disrupted. These acts not only caused material damage to the occupiers but also played a vital psychological role, boosting the morale of the French people and undermining the authority of the Nazis.

In time, some resistance fighters made the decision to join Allied forces fighting in other theatres of the war. These brave individuals crossed enemy lines, often at significant personal risk, to provide intelligence, participate in guerrilla warfare, or join regular military units. Their contribution was invaluable, as they brought a wealth of knowledge and experience from their involvement in the resistance.

The formation of French resistance networks was not without its challenges. Collaboration and betrayal were constant concerns, as some individuals succumbed to the pressures of Nazi intimidation or sought personal gain. The risk of infiltration by Nazi spies added an element of constant danger, forcing resistance groups to be perpetually vigilant. Despite these dangers, the resistance fighters remarkably persevered, trusting in their cause and their ability to overcome adversity.

The relentless efforts of the French resistance finally paid off when the Allied forces, buoyed by their intelligence and support, launched the D-Day invasion in June 1944. The resistance played a critical role in aiding the invasion, facilitating key strategic manoeuvres and helping secure beachheads. Their formidable contribution allowed the liberation of France to unfold swiftly, marking a turning point in the war and signalling the beginning of the end for the Nazi regime.

The formation of French resistance networks is a testament to the human spirit's indomitable will to fight for freedom. It serves as a reminder that even in the darkest times, ordinary people possess extraordinary potential to stand up against tyranny, defend their values, and shape history. The courage and determination displayed by the resistance fighters will forever inspire future generations, symbolising the triumph of resilience over oppression and the enduring power of unity and collective action.

Research and Further Reading References:

Some of the most notable scholarly works that examine the call to arms and the formation of French Resistance networks during the Nazi occupation include:

1. "The Resistance: The French Fight Against the Nazis" by Matthew Cobb, published by Simon & Schuster in 2009, which gives a detailed account of the French Resistance's origins and operations.

2. "Army of Shadows: The History of the French Resistance" by Joseph Kessel, initially published in 1943 and later reissued by Gallimard in 2011 (in French as "L'Armée des ombres"), is a contemporary account by a member of the Resistance but has been treated seriously by scholars due to its firsthand perspective.

3. "Sisters in the Resistance: How Women Fought to Free France, 1940-1945" by Margaret Collins Weitz, published by Wiley in 1995, centres on women's roles in the French Resistance.

4. "A History of the French Resistance" by Gérard Chauvy, published by Editions Perrin in 2019 (in French as "Histoire de la Résistance"), provides a comprehensive exploration of the Resistance's diverse movements and figures.

5. "Unlikely Warriors: The British in the Spanish Civil War and the Struggle Against Fascism" by Richard Baxell, published by Aurum Press in 2012, which, while focused on Britain and Spain, sheds light on pre-war anti-fascist sentiments that fed into the French Resistance.

These works provide insights into the resistance's mobilisation, organisation, and the various groups and individuals who played a part in its formation and activities.

V

Living Under Occupation: Fear and Collusion

As the Nazi occupation tightened its grip on France, the civilian population found themselves thrust into a world of fear, uncertainty, and treacherous choices. The occupation brought about a climate of oppression, surveillance, and collaboration that permeated every aspect of daily life. In this chapter, we delve deep into the experiences of ordinary French citizens as they navigated the challenges of living under occupation.

Fear became an ever-present companion for the people of France during the dark days of Nazi occupation. The brutal tactics employed by the German forces instilled a deep sense of dread as the population lived under the constant threat of violence and persecution. The German military, along with their French collaborators within the milice, subjected the populace to a merciless regime of arbitrary arrests, interrogations, and summary executions that sought to stifle any form of opposition.

Every action, every decision, and every word spoken in public had to be carefully calculated to avoid arousing suspicion. Citizens walked on eggshells, acutely aware that any misstep or perceived defiance could result in dire consequences for themselves and their loved ones. The

Gestapo's pervasive presence, strategically positioned throughout the occupied territories, ensured that fear cast its shadow over the hearts of the French people.

Yet, within this atmosphere of fear existed a toxic aura of collaboration and betrayal. Neighbours turned against neighbours, friends denounced friends, and communities disintegrated under the pressure to survive. Collaboration with the occupiers became an alluring strategy for some to secure better treatment, privileges, and economic opportunities. It was a Faustian bargain, a decision born out of a primal instinct for self-preservation, but one that further fragmented communities and eroded the trust that once bound them together.

The puppet regime of Vichy France, collaborating with the Nazis, implemented policies that actively advanced the German agenda. The Vichy government's complicity in the deportation of Jews, the enforcement of anti-Semitic laws, and its eagerness to assist the Nazi war machine left deep scars on the nation's collective conscience. The regime's collaboration went beyond mere acquiescence; it actively participated in the persecution and destruction of its citizens.

However, it is essential to recognise that not all French citizens succumbed to fear and collaboration. Within the shadows and secret corners of occupied France, an undercurrent of resistance surged— standing as a beacon of hope and defiance against the occupiers. These heroic individuals and groups, known as the Resistance, risked their lives to resist and sabotage the Nazi regime. They provided aid and shelter to those persecuted, disseminated clandestine newspapers to counter propaganda, and carried out acts of sabotage to hinder German operations.

Living under occupation took its toll on the mental and emotional well-being of the French population. The constant surveillance and fear of retribution shattered the social fabric of communities. Trust evaporated, replaced by suspicion and paranoia. Individuals lived in a perpetual state of anticipation, their lives shadowed by the fear that a trusted friend or neighbour may ultimately betray them to the authorities.

The occupation also exacted a heavy toll on the economy, as resources were redirected to support the German war machine. Rationing, scarcity, and widespread poverty became harsh realities for many French citizens. A daily struggle for survival gripped the population as they grappled with food shortages, limited access to healthcare, and a crumbling infrastructure. But even in the face of such dire circumstances, acts of solidarity and resistance emerged.

Underground markets, organised by the black market, became a lifeline for many, allowing the exchange of otherwise scarce or heavily regulated goods. These markets operated discreetly, with secret codes and covert networks keeping them hidden from the prying eyes of the German authorities. Smuggling became common, as individuals risked their lives to bring in essentials such as food, medicine, and fuel. The black market, though fraught with danger and subject to arbitrary enforcement, provided a means for survival and a way to resist the oppression of the occupation.

Within occupied territories, ordinary citizens stepped up to challenge the occupiers in various ways. Some joined the armed resistance ranks, engaging in sabotage, assassinations, and guerrilla warfare against German forces and their collaborators. These brave fighters operated from hidden bases, using their knowledge of local terrain and clandestine networks to strike swift and effective blows against the occupiers.

Others engaged in civil disobedience, subverting German authority through nonviolent means. They boycotted collaborationist businesses, sabotaged German propaganda, and disseminated leaflets and underground newspapers that exposed the truth behind the Nazi regime's atrocities. These acts of resistance were not limited to urban areas alone, as rural communities formed their networks to aid fugitives, shelters, and escape routes, offering a lifeline to those hunted by the occupation forces.

The resilience of the French people in the face of oppression and collaboration stands as a testament to the indomitable human spirit. The heroism and sacrifices of those who resisted the occupiers symbolised their refusal to bow down to tyranny and served as a beacon of hope for future generations. Through their actions, they proved that even in the darkest of times, the flame of liberty can never be extinguished, and the pursuit of freedom is worth risking everything.

Research and Further Reading References:

Scholarly works examining the complex nature of life under occupation in France, particularly the aspects of fear and collaboration, include:

1. "Vichy France: Old Guard and New Order, 1940-1944" by Robert O. Paxton, originally published by Alfred A. Knopf in 1972, is a seminal work that explores the Vichy government's collaboration with Nazi Germany.

2. "The Shameful Peace: How French Artists and Intellectuals Survived the Nazi Occupation" by Frederic Spotts, published by Yale University Press in 2008, delves into the experiences and moral quandaries faced by France's cultural elite during the Occupation.

3. "Marianne in Chains: Daily Life in the Heart of France During the German Occupation" by Robert Gildea, published by Macmillan in

2002, offers an in-depth look at the daily life and the varying degrees of acquiescence and resistance within occupied France.

4. "When Paris Went Dark: The City of Light Under German Occupation, 1940-1944" by Ronald C. Rosbottom, published by Little, Brown, and Company in 2014, recounts the impact of the Occupation on Parisians' daily lives, emphasizing the challenges and moral ambiguities they faced.

5. "Occupation: The Ordeal of France 1940-1944" by Ian Ousby, published by Pimlico in 1999, provides a narrative of the mechanisms of collaboration and the occupation's effects on French society.

VI

Urban Warfare: The Parisian Underground

Paris, the iconic city known for its beauty, culture, and art, played a pivotal role in the French Resistance during the Nazi occupation of France. Underneath the bustling city streets, a hidden war was being fought – the war of the resistance. In this chapter, we will delve even deeper into Paris's crucial role in the French Resistance, exploring the diverse underground networks, key figures, and daring operations in the heart of the capital.

The occupation of Paris by the Nazis in June 1940 marked a turning point in the city's history. The bustling metropolis was transformed into a prison, with its inhabitants subjected to the harsh rule of the occupying forces. However, Parisians did not submit quietly; instead, they defiantly resisted and fought back against Nazi oppression.

One of the key figures in the Parisian Underground was Jean Moulin. Known by the codename "Max," Moulin was an inspiring leader who unified various resistance groups under one cohesive banner. His exceptional organisational skills and strategic thinking allowed him to form the National Council of Resistance, effectively merging the efforts of disparate factions. This unified front became a thorn in the side of the occupying forces and a ray of hope for the oppressed Parisians.

In addition to Moulin, other key figures emerged in the Parisian Underground, each playing a significant role in the resistance movement. Jacques Bingen, an architect by profession, utilised his knowledge of the city's layout to hide resistance members and smuggle information. Raymond Aubrac, a chemical engineer, masterminded numerous daring prison breaks, helping fellow resistance fighters escape the clutches of the Gestapo. Marie-Madeleine Fourcade, a brave woman driven by her patriotism, skillfully ran a vast espionage network known as Alliance from within Paris.

The Parisian Underground was not merely confined to secretive meetings and discussions; it also involved daring acts of resistance and audacious operations. One such operation was the Liberation of Paris in August 1944. As Allied forces advanced towards the city, Parisians seized the opportunity and rose against their oppressors. The resistance fighters and the Free French Forces led by General Charles de Gaulle engaged in fierce urban warfare to liberate the city street by street. The Parisian Underground played an integral role in supplying crucial intelligence, sabotaging German operations, and organising acts of sabotage.

Beneath the bustling city, a hidden labyrinth of tunnels and sewers gave the resistance fighters a vital resource. These covert networks became secret meeting places, hiding spots, and escape routes for the brave individuals who stood against the Nazis. The intricate underground passages allowed the resistance to move undetected, evade capture, and carry out their operations, keeping the flame of resistance alive.

Intelligence gathering and transmission were essential to the Parisian Underground's resistance efforts. Brave members risked their lives infiltrating German-controlled buildings, intercepting messages, and relaying vital information to the Allies. They operated in complete secrecy, utilising hidden rooms, secret codes, and ingenious disguises to gather intelligence that could potentially tip the scales in favour of the liberation effort.

The Parisian Underground also played a crucial role in providing logistical support for the French Resistance. Weapons, supplies, and forged identification papers were smuggled underground and distributed to resistance fighters across the city. These underground networks became the lifeline for the resistance, ensuring their continued resilience against the occupying forces.

However, the perilous nature of the Parisian Underground cannot be understated. The Gestapo and French collaborators relentlessly hunted down resistance fighters, leading to brutal acts of reprisal. The risk of arrest, torture, and execution hung over the heads of those involved in the resistance. Yet, their determination and unwavering commitment to the cause pushed them to endure these dangers and continue the fight for freedom.

The Parisian Underground serves as a testament to the bravery and resilience of the Parisian people during one of the darkest periods in their history. Through their courageous actions, they played a significant role in the eventual liberation of Paris and contributed to the overall spirit of resistance throughout France. The stories of heroism, sacrifice, and unwavering spirit that unfolded within the Parisian Underground will forever be remembered and inspire current and future generations.

Research and Further Reading References:

For scholarship related to urban warfare and the Parisian underground during the Nazi occupation, see the following works:

1. "Paris Under the Occupation" by Jean-Paul Sartre, originally written in 1944 and republished at various intervals, offers contemporary reflections on the experience of living in occupied Paris.

2. "Le Paris des étrangers depuis 1945" (Paris of the foreigners since 1945) by Nancy L. Green, published by Publications de la Sorbonne in 1989, includes discussions relevant to the experience of diverse groups in Paris during and after the occupation.

3. "Occupation: The Ordeal of France 1940-1944" by Ian Ousby, published by Pimlico in 1999, while not exclusively focused on urban warfare, provides a comprehensive view of the occupation's challenges, including in urban centres like Paris.

4. "The Liberation of Paris: How Eisenhower, de Gaulle, and Von Choltitz Saved the City of Light" by Jean Edward Smith, published by Simon & Schuster in 2019, looks at the military and political manoeuvres leading to Paris's liberation, an event closely tied to urban resistance activities.

5. Paris résistant (French Edition) by Henri Michel. ALBIN MICHEL (1 Jan. 1982).

6. Paris allemand by Henri Michel. Albin Michel (1 Jan. 1981).

For a specific focus on urban warfare or the Parisian underground's workings, detailed military histories or specialised studies of the French resistance, often within broader works on World War II, may provide insight. Archival material from museums such as the Musée de la Libération de Paris (Paris Liberation Museum) can also be an essential resource for understanding the intricacies of urban resistance during the occupation.

GEW REPORTS AND ANALYSES TEAM

VII

The Maquis: Rural Guerrilla Fighters

The Maquis, derived from the French word for underbrush, embodied the spirit of resistance against German occupation during World War II. Operating covertly from hidden hideouts in the forests, mountains, and remote areas of France, these rural guerrilla fighters waged a relentless war against the oppressors, leaving an indelible mark on history.

The roots of the Maquis can be traced back to the early days of the occupation when individuals disillusioned by the collaborationist Vichy government sought alternative ways to oppose the Nazis. Escaping forced labour conscription, these defiant souls retreated to the rugged and inhospitable countryside, forming small groups that would evolve into the formidable Maquis.

The men and women who joined the ranks of the Maquis came from diverse backgrounds. Some were former soldiers disillusioned by the defeat of France, while others were passionate young individuals who had seen firsthand the atrocities committed under Nazi rule. Together, they shared a common goal: to reclaim their land, restore liberty, and avenge the suffering of their compatriots.

Survival in the Maquis demanded an array of skills. The harsh conditions of the wilderness required them to adapt quickly to their surroundings, foraging for food and hiding from German patrols. Acutely aware that the occupying forces would relentlessly hunt them down, the resistance fighters had to be adaptable, resourceful, and cautious. They established complex support networks with local communities who risked their lives to provide food, shelter, and valuable information. The symbiotic relationship between the Maquis and these courageous civilians became the backbone of their operations, instilling hope and unity in the face of adversity.

Communication between the Maquis and the broader resistance network was dangerous. The German occupation forces maintained a constant watch for any suspicious activity. Consequently, the resistance fighters resorted to various clandestine methods to relay information. Codes, hidden messages, and using cryptic symbols became the lifeblood of their operation. They developed a language, using simple phrases to convey hidden meanings. Anonymous couriers carrying vital intelligence bravely navigated through enemy lines, their bravery shining as they risked their lives for the cause. Often operating in isolation, these rural fighters relied on their wits, alongside strong bonds of trust and loyalty, to outsmart the enemy.

The Maquis were trailblazers in employing guerrilla warfare tactics, striking with precision and elusiveness. Their intimate knowledge of the local terrain afforded them a strategic advantage, enabling them to ambush German patrols, sabotage infrastructure, and disrupt supply lines. These audacious acts of defiance often came at significant personal risk. Still, they severely hampered the Nazi war machine, throwing it into disarray and bolstering the morale of the French population.

In their unwavering pursuit of freedom, the Maquis also played an instrumental role in aiding and sheltering Allied soldiers and airmen trapped behind enemy lines. Despite the enormous risks, they willingly harboured these individuals, offering them sanctuary and guiding them towards safety. The Maquis' devotion to the cause extended beyond their countrymen, embodying the spirit of international solidarity against tyranny.

The occupiers' brutal tactics repeatedly tested the resolve of the Maquis fighters. The Nazis frequently retaliated against perceived acts of resistance with merciless massacres, the razing of villages, and public executions. Yet, instead of dampening their spirits, these barbaric acts only fuelled the Maquis' determination to fight back and ensure that the sacrifices were not in vain.

The tide began to turn in favour of the French resistance in 1944 as the Allies invaded Normandy. The Maquis eagerly seized this opportunity, coordinating their efforts with the advancing Allied forces. Armed with their invaluable knowledge of the local landscape, they became fierce allies in liberating their homeland, acting as scouts, guides, and combatants. Their assistance proved indispensable, aiding in the swift advancement of the Allies towards victory.

Ultimately, the Maquis' unwavering conviction and willingness to sacrifice everything for the cause paved the way for the liberation of France. Their tenacity, resourcefulness, and ability to strike fear into the hearts of their oppressors left an indelible mark on the nation's history. The Maquis stand as a testament to the enduring power of the human spirit, inspiring future generations to fight for justice, liberty, and the preservation of peace.

Though dispersed across the French countryside, the Maquis formed a network that extended far beyond their units. The interconnectedness of the resistance movement ensured that information flowed, enabling them to coordinate larger-scale sabotages and attacks on high-value targets. Collaborating with other resistance factions, such as the urban-based French Forces of the Interior (FFI), they created a formidable force against the occupying German forces.

One of the greatest strengths of the Maquis was their ability to adapt to their surroundings and sustain themselves in the wilderness. With limited resources, they became masters of survival, using whatever they could find in their natural surroundings. Foraging for food, constructing shelters from natural materials, and fabricating weapons from scrap metal and discarded munitions became skills every Maquisard acquired. The ability to blend seamlessly into their environment allowed them to remain elusive and strike unexpectedly, leaving the enemy in constant instability.

The Maquis' acts of resistance extended beyond confrontation with German soldiers. They actively engaged in acts of subversion, spreading information and propaganda to undermine the occupiers' authority. Through clandestine printing presses and sympathetic editors, they produced and distributed underground newspapers, leaflets, and posters to counteract German propaganda and bolster support for the resistance cause. Their determination to keep the spirit of resistance alive drove them to find innovative ways to communicate their messages effectively continually.

Despite the inherent dangers and the constant threat of betrayal, the Maquis inspired widespread admiration and support among the French population. They were seen as symbols of hope, embodying the unwavering spirit of resistance against a seemingly invincible enemy. Impacted by their courage and determination, local communities rallied around the Maquis, providing them invaluable support and intelligence. Farmers, shopkeepers, and villagers from all walks of life offered safe houses, food, and supplies, risking their own lives. The Maquis' ability to rally the support of the French people played a pivotal role in their survival and success.

Despite overwhelming odds, the Maquis had their share of setbacks and losses. Many brave fighters paid the ultimate price for their defiance, sacrificing their lives for the cause they believed in. However, their sacrifice was not in vain. The Maquis' relentless resistance demoralised and depleted the occupying German forces, diverting substantial resources and attention away from the main fronts of the war. They chipped away at the enemy's resolve, enabling the Allies to proceed with their strategic plans with greater advantage.

The Maquis represent a crucial chapter in the story of World War II, embodying the unwavering spirit of resistance against oppression and tyranny. Their incredible sacrifices and achievements serve as a reminder that even in the darkest of times, ordinary individuals can rise to extraordinary heights. The indomitable spirit of the Maquis lives on as a timeless inspiration, reminding us of our duty to fight for justice, liberty, and the dignity of all humanity.

Research and Further Reading References:

Here are a few of the most notable scholarly works on the French Maquis rural resistance fighters during World War II:

1. Histoire de la Resistance en France, by Henri Michel, includes the Maquis networks and operations coverage. It is still considered one of the definitive works on the topic. Presses Universitaires de France - PUF (1 Nov. 1992).

2. Chronique de la Résistance, La Seconde Guerre mondiale. 2 volumes. French edition by Henri Michel, Alain Guérin. Omnibus (7 Nov. 2002).

3. "The Maquis: A History of the French Resistance Movement" by Julian Jackson. Published in 1976 (Robert Hale Ltd), provides important context on how the Maquis emerged and their tactics against the German occupiers.

4. "The Maquis in History" edited by H.R. Kedward and Roger Austin. A collection of essays from leading historians published in 1976 exploring different aspects of the Maquis movement regionally and nationally.

5. "The French Resistance 1940-1944" by Roderick Kedward. Published in 1975, analyzes the development and impact of the Maquis through a political and social history lens.

6. "Underground in France: Resistance and Reprisals, 1940-1944" by H.R. Kedward. Focuses specifically on Maquis activities in the Dordogne region based on archival research. Published in 1991 by The Dovecote Press.

I've focused on scholarly books published in English that provide overviews supported by archival research on this critical chapter of the French resistance during the Nazi occupation. Let me know if you need any other recommendations.

VIII

Secret Communication: Codes, Ciphers, and Underground Networks

During the dark days of Nazi occupation, communication between members of the French Resistance was not a simple task. The occupying forces closely monitored mail, telephone lines, and other conventional means of communication, making resistance fighters rely on secret codes, cyphers, and underground networks to transmit their messages.

Codes and cyphers became essential tools for preserving secrecy and ensuring the safety of resistance members. One of the most widely used methods was the substitution cypher, where each letter of the alphabet was replaced by another letter or symbol. However, relying solely on substitution cyphers had its limitations. The Nazis, with their advanced cryptanalysis techniques, could break many of these codes with time and resources. Therefore, resistance networks began using more complex cyphers, such as the Vigenère cypher, which used a keyword as its basis for encryption. Each keyword letter would determine the shift in the substitution cypher, making it much more difficult to decipher without the keyword.

To transmit coded messages, resistance fighters would use everyday items such as newspapers or letters, marking specific letters or words to convey their real meaning. These markings could be as subtle as an underlined word or a tiny dot next to a specific letter. Only those with the corresponding cypher key who knew how to decipher these hidden markings could reveal the valid message.

To further complicate matters, resistance networks often developed unique codes and cyphers, ensuring that the others would remain secure even if one network were compromised. These custom codes relied on shared knowledge among resistance members, including hidden meanings within everyday phrases, common acronyms, or personal codes only known to a select few. Some resistance members even created their secret languages, filled with invented words and phrases, adding a layer of complexity to communication.

Underground networks played a vital role in facilitating communication within the resistance. These elaborate networks allowed messages and supplies to be transported secretly across the country. They operated strictly need-to-know, with only a few individuals aware of the complete network's structure. This compartmentalisation reduced the risk of one person possessing too much information and being forced to reveal it under interrogation or torture.

The underground networks maintained safe houses where resistance members could gather, receive updates, and transmit messages in a secure environment. These safe houses were often abandoned or inconspicuous buildings, meticulously chosen to avoid drawing suspicion. Inside, resistance members would find hidden compartments, false walls, and concealed compartments within everyday objects to store their codes, cyphers, and equipment. These safe houses became fortresses of hope and determination, where resistance fighters gathered, strategised, and strengthened their resolve.

In addition to traditional methods, technology played a significant part in communication within the resistance. Radio transmitters became tools of utmost importance, enabling messages to be broadcast anonymously and rapidly across vast territories. These transmitters were small, portable devices that could be easily hidden or moved to avoid detection by the occupiers. Radio operators, skilled in using these devices, would encode messages and transmit them using predetermined frequencies, ensuring they reached their intended recipients. These messages provided resistance fighters with crucial information, such as locations of key Nazi installations, details about troop movements, and updates on allied operations.

The coordination of secret communication was a complex and delicate task. Safeguarding these communication channels was crucial to the success of the resistance's various operations. One breach could lead to the capture, arrest, and even execution of resistance members, endangering the entire movement. Therefore, the codes, cyphers, and underground networks had to continuously adapt and evolve to stay one step ahead of the occupying forces.

Resistance members used various methods to test the security of their communication channels. They would employ individuals known as "double agents," whose primary role was to attempt to infiltrate the network under the guise of collaboration with the Nazis. These double agents would pass intercepted messages, pretending they were still loyal to the resistance, to determine if anyone within the network had been compromised. The resilience of the resistance lay not only in their ability to keep their secrets hidden but also in their vigilance in weeding out potential traitors.

The importance of secret communication cannot be overstated in the story of the French Resistance. These clandestine methods of conveying information played a vital role in coordinating acts of sabotage, sharing intelligence, and maintaining the spirit of resistance and hope in occupied France. The individuals who meticulously crafted and transmitted these messages, and those who risked their lives to deliver them, are unsung heroes in the annals of history, their significant and inspiring contributions. It is through their courage and determination that the French Resistance became a force to be reckoned with and ultimately played a crucial role in the liberation of France from Nazi occupation.

Within these underground networks, another element played a vital role in maintaining the communication channels—the couriers. These brave individuals would risk their lives as they travelled through enemy territory to deliver messages, codes, and cyphers to resistance cells and safe houses across the country. Couriers had exceptional knowledge of the land, using their familiarity with the terrain and cunning to avoid detection. They would often travel on foot or by bicycle, relying on the cover of darkness and the shadows to slip past Nazi checkpoints and patrols unnoticed.

The selection and training of couriers were meticulous processes. Candidates were chosen based on their physical fitness, resilience, and dedication to the cause. These individuals underwent rigorous training in navigation, survival skills, and evasion tactics. They were tasked with memorising the intricate network of safe houses, codes, and contacts, ready to traverse miles on foot or bicycle to deliver their critical payloads.

The couriers' missions were wrought with danger and uncertainty. The risk of capture or betrayal was ever-present, and the consequences of failure were grave. If caught, couriers faced brutal interrogations and torture, with the Nazis attempting to extract information about the resistance network and its members. Many couriers faced imprisonment, while others, tragically, met their end at the hands of their captors.

To maximise their chances of success, couriers would embark on their missions alone or in small groups, diminishing the chances of drawing attention. They would often travel through treacherous terrain, such as dense forests or mountainous regions, where they could rely on the cover of nature to shield their movements from prying eyes. Some would disguise themselves as civilian workers or farmers, blending into their surroundings and avoiding suspicion as they navigated checkpoints and military installations.

Couriers also relied on the support of sympathetic French citizens who provided them with safe houses, food, and shelter along their perilous journeys. These brave individuals formed an extensive network of helpers, willing to risk their lives and the safety of their families in the fight against Nazi oppression. Acting as intermediaries between resistance cells, these citizens played an integral role in ensuring the success of the communication network. Their silent acts of solidarity and bravery allowed the messages of resistance to flow, strengthening the bonds between different cells and spreading hope throughout occupied France.

As the war dragged on, the French Resistance's secret communication network faced increasing pressure from the Nazi occupiers. The occupying forces employed skilled cryptanalysts and intelligence personnel to decipher and disrupt resistance messages. The resistance was countered by employing expert code-makers, constantly developing new cyphers, and refining their codes to stay ahead of the Nazi efforts.

Among these code-makers, one name stands out: Jean-Pierre Leclerc. Leclerc was a brilliant mathematician with a natural talent for codebreaking and cryptography. As a member of the resistance, he played a crucial role in developing complex cyphers and encryption methods to protect the communication channels of the French Resistance.

Leclerc's codes were known for their sophistication and effectiveness. He would often combine multiple encryption techniques, creating layers of complexity that would require a great deal of time and resources to decipher. One of his most famous creations was a polyalphabetic cypher that he called "Leclerc's Lockbox." This cypher utilised a rotating alphabet system, where the shifted alphabets would change with each letter of the message. It was a highly secure method that proved to be nearly impossible for the Nazis to crack.

Leclerc also developed an innovative method of transmitting coded messages using invisible ink. He would write his messages in lemon juice, which would become visible when exposed to heat or certain chemicals. This allowed resistance fighters to hide their messages in plain sight on seemingly innocent pieces of paper. Resistance members would write a seemingly ordinary letter or correspondence to transmit the messages, with the hidden message written using invisible ink. The recipient would then use the appropriate method to reveal and decode the hidden message.

In addition to his skills in cryptography, Leclerc was also responsible for training and instructing other resistance members in secret communication. He taught them the intricacies of his cyphers, encryption techniques, and the importance of maintaining secrecy and vigilance in constant surveillance. Leclerc's expertise and dedication to the cause greatly enhanced the resistance's ability to effectively communicate and coordinate their operations.

Despite the risks and challenges they faced, the secret communication methods of the French Resistance proved to be invaluable throughout the occupation. The resistance's ability to maintain its network and transmit critical information played a crucial role in the success of its operations. It allowed them to coordinate acts of sabotage, gather intelligence, and keep the spirit of resistance alive even in the face of overwhelming odds.

The codes, cyphers, and underground networks of the French Resistance serve as a testament to the power of human ingenuity and determination. In the face of oppression and adversity, ordinary individuals found extraordinary ways to protect their messages and preserve their cause. Their secret communication methods ensured that the flame of resistance remained burning, inspiring future generations to stand up against injustice and fight for freedom.

The legacy of the French Resistance lives on as a symbol of bravery, resilience, and the power of unity. Their secret communication methods continue to inspire cryptographers and code-breakers, reminding us of cryptography's critical role in preserving privacy, security, and the freedom to dissent. The stories of these unsung heroes serve as a reminder that even in the darkest times, there is always a glimmer of hope and the potential for ordinary individuals to make an extraordinary impact.

Research and Further Reading References:

The following scholarly works provide in-depth insights into these clandestine activities:

1. "Battle of Wits: The Complete Story of Codebreaking in World War II" by Stephen Budiansky, published in 2000 by Simon and Schuster. This book provides a comprehensive overview of the role of codebreaking during World War II, including activities in France.
2. "Codebreakers: The Inside Story of Bletchley Park" by F. H. Hinsley and Alan Stripp, published in 2001 by Oxford University Press. This work details the efforts of the British codebreaking

centre at Bletchley Park, which had significant connections with the French resistance.

3.   "Codebreakers' Victory: How the Allied Cryptographers Won World War II" by Hervie Haufler, published in 2014 by Open Road Media. This book highlights the contributions of Allied cryptographers, including their interactions with and support for the French resistance.

4.   "Outwitting the Gestapo" by Lucie Aubrac, translated by Konrad Bieber and Betsy Wing, published in 1994 by the University of Nebraska Press. This personal account provides an intimate view of the resistance movement in France, including the use of secret communications to evade and undermine the Nazi occupation.

5.   "The French Resistance: 1940–1944" by Raymond and Lucie Aubrac, published in 1997 by Hazan Editeur in Paris. This book offers an insider perspective on the French Resistance, discussing various tactics, including secret communications.

6.   "Silent Heroes: Downed Airmen and the French Underground" by Sherri Greene Ottis, published in 2001 by the University of Kentucky Press. It details the network that supported downed airmen, including the use of codes and secret messages.

7.   "Occupation" by Ian Ousby, published in 2000 by Cooper Square Press. This work provides a broader context of the Nazi occupation of France, within which these secret communications networks operated.

8.   "Sisters in the Resistance: How Women Fought to Free France, 1940–1945" by Margaret Collins Weitz, published in 1998 by John Wiley & Sons. This book focuses on the role of women in the French Resistance, including their involvement in secret communication efforts.

IX

Acts of Sabotage: Disrupting the Nazi War Machine

In the face of Nazi occupation, the French Resistance recognised the need to take action against the German war machine. Acts of sabotage became a crucial strategy employed by the resistance fighters to disrupt German operations, hamper their supply chains, and strike fear into the hearts of the occupying forces.

Sabotage took many forms, encompassing a wide range of actions that required careful planning, resourcefulness, and bravery. The diverse array of individuals involved in the resistance, including Communists, liberals, nationalists, and ordinary citizens, brought different skills and perspectives to the table, contributing to the effectiveness of sabotage efforts.

Blowing up railway lines and bridges was a highly effective method of sabotage. Resistance fighters, known as "train wreckers," carefully studied German supply routes and targeted crucial points to disrupt transportation and halt the flow of troops and supplies. These acts caused immediate disruptions and created long-term logistical challenges for the German war effort.

Resistance members often face immense danger in carrying out these acts. They had to work quickly, under cover of darkness, digging holes beneath the tracks, positioning explosives, and then making a swift escape. Bombs were set to detonate at unsuspecting moments, ensuring a maximum impact. The train wreckers displayed remarkable courage, determination, and meticulous planning despite the risks involved.

Communication networks were also a frequent target of sabotage. Resistance members cut telephone lines, intercepted German messages, and planted false information to mislead the enemy. This sophisticated intelligence gathering and deception operation was crucial in undermining the Germans' ability to coordinate their operations effectively.

Resistance fighters tapped into their technical expertise, using homemade radios to intercept enemy transmissions. They deciphered codes, monitored German troop movements, and fed vital information to the Allies. These sabotage acts disrupted German communication and provided valuable intelligence to the resistance network, enabling them to plan future operations more effectively.

Sabotaging German weapons and ammunition depots was another important tactic employed by the resistance. These facilities were vital for the enemy's military capabilities, and their destruction deprived the Germans of vital resources and created delays in their ability to replenish armaments. The resistance fighters understood the significance of disrupting supply chains and reducing the effectiveness of the enemy's firepower.

Courageous members of the resistance infiltrated military installations, risking their lives to place explosive charges. They targeted warehouses filled with weapons and ammunition, setting off a chain reaction of destruction. These daring acts not only caused immediate damage but also sowed doubt within the German ranks, as they questioned the security of their own installations and the reliability of their collaborators.

Urban guerrilla tactics were also utilised, with bombings and assassinations aimed at key German officials and collaborators. These actions eliminated prominent figures and created a sense of fear and paranoia among the occupying forces and their collaborators. This psychological impact further weakened the enemy's grip and served as a rallying call for the French people.

Resistance fighters, often working in small groups known as maquis, conducted targeted attacks on German officers and collaborators. These courageous individuals expertly blended into the urban landscape, striking swiftly and disappearing into the chaos of the city. They demonstrated exceptional marksmanship and precision, choosing their targets carefully to deliver decisive blows to the enemy's morale.

Underneath the audacious acts of sabotage and guerrilla warfare, the resistance relied on a vast network of ordinary citizens who quietly played essential roles. They provided the resistance fighters safe houses, intelligence, supplies, and transportation. These courageous individuals were the unsung heroes who risked their lives to support the resistance and ensure its operations could continue.

Quiet heroes such as Jean Moulin, a key figure in unifying the resistance, coordinated the efforts of various resistance groups, ensuring they worked toward a common goal. Moulin's leadership and tenacity provided direction and a sense of unity among the resistance fighters, solidifying their determination to fight against German occupation.

The risks faced by the resistance members cannot be overstated. Gestapo agents and collaborators were actively hunting down fighters, and betrayal from within their own ranks was a constant threat.

Interrogations, torture, and death awaited those captured by the enemy. Nevertheless, the resistance persevered. They were driven by a deep desire for freedom, an unwavering commitment to their country, and a belief in the righteousness of their cause.

The sabotage acts carried out by the French Resistance were not isolated incidents. They were part of a broader strategy designed to erode the confidence of the German occupiers and undermine their control over France. The resistance aimed to create an atmosphere of uncertainty and fear, making the enemy question their ability to maintain their hold on the occupied territory.

Beyond the immediate disruptions caused, the sabotage conducted by the French Resistance had a profound impact on the Nazi war machine. It significantly hindered German operations, slowed their ability to deploy troops and supplies, and disrupted communication and logistical networks. These actions not only served as a physical hindrance but also dealt a psychological blow to the occupiers, as they realised the resilience and determination of the French people.

The legacy of the acts of sabotage carried out by the French Resistance during the Nazi occupation continues to be felt today. They stand as a reminder of the indomitable human spirit and collective action's power against tyranny. The resistance fighters and their supporters displayed extraordinary courage, resourcefulness, and unwavering dedication to a cause greater than themselves. Their actions serve as a testament to the strength of the human spirit and the triumph of resistance in the face of oppression.

Research and Further Reading References:

Several scholarly works provide valuable insights into acts of sabotage against the Nazi war machine in occupied France during World War II. The resistance carried out sabotage activities like derailing trains, damaging factories and infrastructure, and hindering German troop movements to disrupt the Nazi war effort.

1.   Smith, Meredith. *The Civilian Experience in German-Occupied France.* No. 6, 1940, digitalcommons.conncoll.edu/cgi/viewcontent.cgi?article=1005&context=histhp. This 2010 journal article examines civilian experiences in occupied France, noting acts of sabotage increased through the war, especially targeting the railways. It highlights railway worker strikes and go-slows that effectively delayed German troop and supply movements before D-Day.

2.   Wegner, Larissa. "Occupation during the War (Belgium and France) | International Encyclopedia of the First World War (WW1)." *1914-1918-Online.net*, 2014, encyclopedia.1914-1918-online.net/article/occupation_during_the_war_belgium_and_france. This 2014 encyclopedia entry details German policies and practices in occupied France and Belgium. It notes the resistance focused sabotage on transport networks and industrial centres to slow war production and troop movements before the Normandy invasion.

3.   On Strike Against the Nazis, By Steve Cushion and Merilyn Moos. Socialist History. Occasional Publication 47. The Socialist History Society, 2021: This 97-page publication analyses the French communist party's shift to active resistance after Germany invaded the Soviet Union in 1941. It discusses communist-led sabotage of factories, infrastructure, and troop transports in northern France: https://discovery.ucl.ac.uk/id/eprint/10159400/1/On-strike.pdf

4. Resistance: The Underground War Against Hitler, 1939-1945, By Halik KochanskiLiveright (2022). This book examines resistance activities across Nazi-occupied Europe. It highlights the pre-D-Day sabotage of transport and communication networks in France, which was planned in coordination with the Allied invasion.

5. Smith, McKay M. "Bearing Silent Witness: A Grandfather's Secret Attestation to German War Crimes in Occupied France." Journal of Strategic Security 6, no. 3 Suppl. (2013): 358-381.

A 1944 military report analyses German sabotage efforts in the US, noting they pale compared to resistance sabotage in occupied nations. It states such sabotage was key to reducing Germany's capacity and will to resist. https://digitalcommons.usf.edu/cgi/viewcontent.cgi?article=1686&context=jss

X

Intelligence Gathering: Spies and Informants

During the dark days of Nazi occupation in France, intelligence gathering played a crucial role in the underground resistance movement. Spies and informants risked their lives to provide valuable information to the resistance networks, helping them undermine the German occupiers and contribute to the eventual liberation of France.

One of the primary sources of intelligence for the resistance was the vast network of informants spread throughout France. These individuals, motivated by a strong belief in freedom and their desire to see the Nazis defeated, came from different walks of life. They included shopkeepers, journalists, teachers, factory workers, and railway employees who had access to key information due to their interactions with German soldiers, government officials, or within their respective industries. These informants discreetly passed on details about German troop movements, supply routes, and other sensitive information that could be utilised to plan acts of sabotage or other resistance operations. Code names were often used to protect their sources and maintain secrecy, allowing for anonymity and reducing the risk of exposure.

The resistance also relied on undercover agents, commonly known as spies, who infiltrated German-controlled areas or Nazi organisations to gather intelligence. These individuals possessed a remarkable skill set that allowed them to blend seamlessly into their surroundings while doing clandestine work. Some spies assumed false identities and fabricated intricate backstories to play the role of collaborators or sympathisers convincingly. They worked close to German officials, eavesdropping on conversations and secretly collecting documents that held invaluable information. These spies went to great lengths to gain the trust of the occupiers and gather valuable information, risking their lives every day to contribute to the resistance efforts.

The resistance developed elaborate systems of coded messages and hidden signals to communicate with their informants and spies. These covert communication methods were crucial for protecting the identity of their sources and ensuring that the information gathered reached the right hands. Resistance members sometimes utilised invisible ink, microdots, or even cryptic symbols to convey their messages. Decoding these messages required extensive training and specific knowledge shared only among trusted resistance members.

The meticulousness required in intelligence gathering was matched by the bravery and resourcefulness of those involved. Resistance fighters often built secret hideouts and used innovative techniques to evade detection by the German authorities. They developed strategies to keep their activities covert, such as taking different routes and using dead letter drops to exchange information without direct contact. In some cases, individuals would even carry false identification papers or engage in acts of petty crime to create alibis for their hidden roles in the resistance.

However, the work of intelligence gathering was rife with risks and challenges. The Nazis employed a vast network of informants themselves, making it difficult for the resistance to separate friend from foe. The Gestapo, the German secret police, used fear and intimidation to coerce individuals into betraying the resistance, creating an atmosphere of constant suspicion. To counter this threat, resistance groups implemented rigorous vetting processes to assess the trustworthiness of potential informants and spies. These processes involved extensive background cheques, evaluations of character, and recruitment through trusted intermediaries. While not foolproof, these measures provided some level of confidence in those providing crucial intelligence to the resistance.

The repercussions for being caught gathering or providing intelligence were severe – imprisonment, torture, or even death awaited those who were discovered. This constant threat placed immense pressure on the resistance members gathering information and those processing it, emphasising the importance of trust and secrecy within the networks. The resistance developed elaborate escape plans and fallback positions to ensure the safety of operatives if they were compromised. These plans considered alternative identities, safe houses, and emergency escape routes that resistance members could rely on in dire situations.

In many cases, intelligence gathering went hand in hand with acts of sabotage. Resistance fighters would strike strategically, such as railway lines, factories, or communication hubs, to disrupt the German war effort. The information gathered helped them plan these operations effectively, maximising their chances of success while minimising the risk to innocent lives. This coordination between intelligence gathering and acts of sabotage required meticulous planning and careful execution, with each operation relying on accurate and timely information.

The intelligence-gathering operations conducted by the French resistance not only provided valuable information to the Allies but also served as a demonstration of the resilience and determination of the French people in the face of adversity. Despite the constant threat of discovery and the fear of reprisals, these brave individuals continued to gather intelligence, fuelling hope for eventual liberation.

As we explore the stories of individuals involved in intelligence gathering, we uncover their challenges, triumphs, and sacrifices. Their efforts, often performed in secrecy and at significant personal risk, form an integral part of the broader narrative of resistance against the Nazi occupiers. Their unwavering commitment to the cause reminds us of the power of information and the extraordinary lengths individuals will go to fight for freedom and justice.

In the next chapter, we delve into the complex world of covert operations and the intricate plans devised by the resistance to disrupt the Nazi regime. The French resistance aimed to weaken German control and inspire hope among the oppressed through daring sabotage and calculated attacks on occupied institutions.

Research and Further Reading References:

1. "Sisters in the Resistance: How Women Fought to Free France, 1940-1945". Margaret Collins Weitz. John Wiley & Sons, Inc. 1995.

2. "A Life in Secrets: The Story of Vera Atkins and the Lost Agents of SOE". Sarah Helm. Little, Brown Book Group. 2006.
Note: Provides insight into the Special Operations Executive (SOE) and its networks, including its operations in France.

3. "The Resistance: The French Fight Against the Nazis". Matthew Cobb. Simon & Schuster UK. 2009.
Note: Offers a comprehensive overview of the French resistance, mentioning the intelligence aspect of the movement.

4. "Shadow Warriors: The Covert War in France, D-Day to the Liberation of Paris". William B. Breuer. Presidio Press. 2003.

Note: Focuses on the covert operations, including espionage, that occurred leading up to and following D-Day.

XI

From the Shadows to the Frontline: Resistance Fighters Joining Allied Forces

Throughout the darkest years of Nazi occupation in France, the members of the French Resistance fought fiercely to undermine the enigmatic grip of the occupiers. Their tireless efforts ranged from sabotage to intelligence gathering, all in pursuing one goal: liberation. However, as the war progressed, many resistance fighters felt the need to take their fight to the next level by joining the Allied forces on the frontline. This chapter explores these individuals' motivations, challenges, and heroic endeavours as they transitioned from the shadows of resistance to the harsh realities of war.

For many resistance fighters, joining the Allied forces was a natural progression in their fight against tyranny. The collaboration between resistance groups and the Allied armies not only strengthened the collective effort against the Nazis but also provided individuals with a sense of purpose and camaraderie. By joining the frontline, resistance fighters hoped to directly contribute to the liberation of their homeland and bring an end to the atrocities committed under the Nazi regime.

However, the journey from the clandestine world of resistance to the structured environment of a military unit was not without its challenges. Many resistance fighters had operated in small, independent cells where decisions were made collectively and without hierarchical structure. Transitioning to military life meant submitting to a strict chain of command, following orders, and adhering to military discipline - a significant adjustment for those accustomed to the freedom of action. Yet, despite these challenges, their unwavering determination and adaptability propelled them forward.

One of the key challenges faced by resistance fighters joining the Allied forces was integration. Many of these individuals had lived secretive lives under constant threat of detection, relying on aliases and hidden identities. Now, they had to reveal their true identities and navigate the often complex process of joining the military ranks. This process involved paperwork, medical examinations, and in-depth interviews to assess their skills, experiences, and commitment to the cause. It was a test of their resolve and determination to transition from the shadows to the frontline seamlessly.

Once accepted, resistance fighters found themselves training alongside fellow soldiers from different backgrounds, some of whom were unaware of the secret lives they had led. A delicate balance existed between a desire to share their experiences as part of the resistance and the need to maintain operational security. While some found solace and understanding among fellow veterans of the underground, others felt isolated and struggled to articulate the weight of their experiences to those who had not shared their journey. This internal conflict shaped their interactions with their comrades and highlighted the emotional toll that resistance work had taken on them.

The resilience, adaptability, and strategic thinking of resistance fighters translated well to the harsh realities of war. Once deployed to the frontline, they faced brutal battles, braving the harshest conditions and witnessing the atrocities of war up close. The experience of underground resistance work had honed their survival instincts, making them adept at navigating dangerous situations, often relying on their intuition and quick thinking. They were the unsung heroes, infiltrating enemy lines, gathering crucial intelligence, and participating in specialised operations to weaken the enemy's grip on occupied territories.

Many resistance fighters were deployed as paratroopers, dropping behind enemy lines to disrupt Nazi operations and provide vital support to the advancing Allied forces. Their knowledge of local geography, networks, and infrastructure proved invaluable in targeting key German installations and communication centres. Their clandestine skills, such as sabotage techniques, forgery, and evasion tactics, were honed to perfection, ensuring maximum impact against the occupiers.

Yet, the transition from the clandestine world of resistance to the open theatre of war was not without sacrifice. Many resistance fighters paid the ultimate price, losing their lives in combat or falling victim to Nazi reprisals. Their names may not be widely known, but their unwavering dedication and courage remain etched in the annals of history. Their stories serve as a poignant reminder of the heavy toll war exacts on individuals and the profound impact of the resistance movement on the European landscape.

The bravery and dedication of resistance fighters who joined the Allied forces did not go unnoticed. Their unique skill sets, gained through years of clandestine operations, were valuable to the military. Their understanding of the local landscape, knowledge of enemy activities, and experience in covert operations proved indispensable in the fight against the Nazis. Moreover, their presence on the frontline symbolised hope and resilience, inspiring others to resist and reinforcing the belief that freedom will prevail over oppression.

The stories of resistance fighters transitioning from the shadows to the frontline are a testament to human endurance and determination. Their sacrifice and courage are a reminder of the collective strength that can be achieved when individuals unite for a common cause. They embody the spirit of resistance and remind us all of the resilience of the human spirit, even in the face of unimaginable adversity. Their legacy will forever be intertwined with the struggle for freedom and the triumph of good over evil. Their actions shall serve as an eternal reminder that ordinary individuals can achieve extraordinary feats and that no obstacle is insurmountable when faced with unwavering resolve and the conviction that freedom is worth fighting for.

Research and Further Reading References:

1. François Kersaudy. *De Gaulle et Churchill : La Mésentente Cordiale*. Paris, Éditions Perrin, 2003: explores the relationship between these two key figures during the war, including their interactions with the French Resistance.
2. Cobb, Matthew. *The Resistance*. London, Pocket Books, 2010, offering a detailed examination of the French Resistance's role and activities during World War II.
3. Callil, Carmen. *Bad Faith*. Vintage, 10 Dec. 2008.

XII

Women in the Resistance: Courage and Contribution

Throughout history, women have often found themselves in the shadows, their accomplishments forgotten or undermined. Yet, in the narrative of the French Resistance during World War II, women emerged as exceptional figures, essential and resolute in their fight against Nazi occupation. Their unparalleled bravery, intelligence, and determination shattered traditional gender boundaries and showcased the crucial role of women in the Resistance.

Women faced numerous challenges in their battle against ruthless occupiers in a society primarily dominated by men. Not only did they confront the perils of clandestine operations, but they also had to defy societal norms that pigeonholed them into strictly defined gender roles. Nevertheless, they rose above these obstacles, affirming their indispensability to the success of the Resistance.

A remarkable facet of women's involvement in the Resistance was their adeptness at seamlessly blending into their communities. Capitalising on their roles as mothers, daughters, wives, and workers, they covertly gathered vital information. They became inconspicuous heroes, their acts of defiance and courage often overlooked by the occupying forces.

Women of the Resistance utilised various ingenious methods to gather intelligence. Mothers, posing as ordinary citizens, harnessed their connections at schools, church groups, and other social gatherings to discreetly extract tidbits of information from German soldiers or collaborators. Their keen observational skills and understanding of the power dynamics within their communities allowed them to discern essential details, which they relayed to Resistance leaders.

Female couriers played a pivotal role in maintaining communication networks and ensuring the smooth flow of information among Resistance factions. These women courageously traversed dangerous paths in urban centres and the countryside, acting as invaluable liaisons. By skillfully navigating the clandestine pathways, they carried messages, photographs, and weapons and coordinated the movements of Resistance members. Their ability to blend into the background, often masquerading as everyday individuals, gave them an advantage not easily attainable by their male counterparts.

Moreover, women's remarkable ability to deceive and manipulate proved instrumental to the Resistance's success. Many women took on false identities, assuming roles that allowed them access to vital information or enabled them to infiltrate the enemy. They became experts in the art of subterfuge while partaking in acts of espionage, serving double roles as secretaries, nurses, or even maids in German-occupied buildings. These brave women risked discovery daily, knowing that discovery meant certain death. Yet, they remained resilient, determined to undermine the occupiers and protect their fellow countrymen.

Remarkably, women also took on active combat roles, joining armed Resistance groups and engaging in acts of sabotage. These fearless individuals risked their lives alongside their male comrades, their resilience and courage shining in perilous circumstances. Whether wielding firearms, planting explosives, or engaging in acts of partisan warfare, they proved themselves to be formidable opponents of tyranny. These heroines, fighting shoulder to shoulder with men, shattered the perception of women as weak, demanding recognition and respect for their dedication and valour.

It is crucial to acknowledge that women in the Resistance faced distinct dangers and challenges due to their gender. If captured, they were not only subjected to imprisonment and torture but also endured additional forms of abuse, such as sexual violence. Despite these horrifying prospects, these women pressed on, fully aware of the potential consequences of their actions. Their resilience and unwavering commitment to the cause demonstrated the strength and determination that resided within them.

The contributions of women in the Resistance were immeasurable. In addition to providing vital intelligence, they inspired others to join the fight against Nazi oppression. Their actions defied societal expectations and paved the way for greater gender equality in post-war France. The remarkable stories of these brave women resonate deeply with their roots of fortitude and bravery.

Acknowledging and highlighting their role in the Resistance, we honour their memory and inspire present and future generations to stand against injustice. These incredible women remind us that strength defies gender, and in the face of adversity, every individual possesses the capacity to make a lasting impact. Their legacy is a powerful testament to the indomitable spirit of women, forever woven into the annals of the French Resistance's courageous struggle for freedom.

Research and Further Reading References:

1.   Reid, Donald. *Germaine Tillion, Lucie Aubrac, and the Politics of Memories of the French Resistance.* Cambridge Scholars Publishing, 26 Mar. 2009.

2.   Women in the French Resistance: Revisiting the Historical Record, by Peninah Scheinberg (Journal of Contemporary History, Vol. 47, No. 4, 2012).

3.   "Nursing Clio Women in the French Resistance," by Nursing Clio (Nursing Clio, 2019).

4.   5 Heroic Women of the French Resistance, Sarah Roller.30 May 2023: https://www.historyhit.com/heroic-women-of-the-french-resistance/

5.   Out of the Shadows: Women in the French Resistance" (Alternate Source): The Local France. 2 Mar 2023.
       https://www.thelocal.fr/20230302/out-of-the-shadows-women-in-the-french-resistance

6.   Out of the shadows: women in the French Resistance. (France 24, 2022):
       https://www.france24.com/en/live-news/20230302-out-of-the-shadows-women-in-the-french-resistance

XIII

Espionage and Intelligence

The importance of information gathering and intelligence was paramount to the success of the French Resistance during the Nazi occupation. In this chapter, we will explore the vital role of spies and the crucial work carried out by the Special Operations Executive (SOE).

Information was power, and the Resistance understood the value of obtaining accurate and timely intelligence. Without reliable information, their efforts to sabotage the Nazi war machine and support the Allied forces would have been significantly hampered. The Resistance relied on a network of spies and informants who risked their lives to gather critical details about enemy movements, military plans, and other strategic information.

The SOE, established by the British government in 1940, was central to supporting and coordinating intelligence efforts. Its primary objective was to assist resistance movements in Nazi-occupied territories through espionage, sabotage, and subversion. The SOE became a vital ally to the French Resistance, providing training, resources, and operational guidance.

The SOE trained and deployed agents, often referred to as "spooks" or "pianists," who infiltrated Nazi-controlled areas and operated in secrecy. These agents came from a wide range of backgrounds, including military personnel, linguists, academics, and even ordinary citizens willing to join the fight against the Nazi regime. Their mission was to gather intelligence, recruit local resistance members, and carry out acts of sabotage.

The agents underwent rigorous training in various aspects of espionage and clandestine operations. They were required to learn cryptography, combat techniques, radio communication, and sabotage methods. The SOE also equipped agents with specialised tools, including hidden cameras, miniature radios, and codes for secret communication. These resources allowed agents to blend in with the civilian population and carry out their missions undetected.

The importance of intelligence gathering cannot be overstated. It provided the Resistance with critical information for planning successful sabotage missions, disrupting enemy supply lines, and protecting vulnerable targets. The knowledge obtained through espionage allowed the Resistance to launch coordinated attacks, create diversions, and mitigate the impact of German offensives. The lives of Resistance fighters and innocent civilians often depended on the accuracy and timeliness of the information gathered.

The SOE collaborated closely with local Resistance networks, relying on their knowledge of the area and contacts. This collaboration was essential in building trust and obtaining reliable information. Local Resistance members served as the "eyes and ears" on the ground, providing valuable insights into enemy movements, troop strengths, and strategic targets. They supplied the SOE agents with critical information and liaised between the SOE and the larger Resistance network.

One of the key challenges the Resistance and the SOE faced was the constant threat of infiltration and betrayal. The Gestapo and other Nazi intelligence agencies actively sought to dismantle Resistance networks by planting double agents and using various methods of deception. This created an atmosphere of constant tension and forced the Resistance to exercise extreme caution when sharing sensitive information.

The SOE established stringent security protocols and implemented thorough screening processes to combat this threat. Agents and resistance members underwent extensive vetting, and elaborate codes and

THE FRENCH RESISTANCE AGAINST NAZI OCCUPATION

communication methods were implemented to reduce the risk of compromised information. The SOE trained agents to detect and counter enemy intelligence efforts, emphasising the importance of maintaining operational security. Despite these measures, the constant danger of informants and infiltrators haunted every operation and decision made by the Resistance.

The intelligence gathered by the Resistance and the SOE proved invaluable for the success of the Allied forces. Information related to troop movements, locations of military installations, and weapon supply routes allowed the Resistance, together with the Allied armies, to plan targeted attacks and disrupt Nazi operations. This intelligence was carefully relayed through various channels, often involving coded messages transmitted via disguised radio or couriers.

However, while the role of espionage and intelligence was crucial, it also presented ethical dilemmas for the Resistance fighters. They had to balance the need to obtain critical information with the risk of endangering their own lives and those of innocent civilians. Some Resistance members faced difficult decisions when engaging with Nazi sympathisers or collaborators, as they had to weigh the potential benefit of intelligence against the possibility of betrayal.

Throughout the Nazi occupation, the efforts of the Resistance and the SOE to gather intelligence played a significant role in weakening Nazi control over France. They gave the Allies vital information that helped in strategic decision-making and resource allocation. The information collected by spies and Resistance members also proved essential in preparing for the eventual liberation of France.

*****

The vital role of spies and the crucial work carried out by the Special Operations Executive (SOE) for the success of the French Resistance during the Nazi occupation can be summarised as follows:

- The SOE was established in 1940 by British Prime Minister Winston Churchill to conduct espionage, sabotage and build resistance networks in Nazi-occupied Europe, including France. It recruited and trained agents, including many women, to parachute behind enemy lines and support local resistance groups.

- In France, the SOE helped build one of the largest resistance networks, Alliance, led by Marie-Madeleine Fourcade. Female SOE agents like Noor Inayat Khan and Odette Sansom bravely carried out dangerous missions in France, acting as wireless operators, couriers and more.

- SOE agents provided critical intelligence on German defences, troop movements, supply lines, transport and communication facilities, which was vital for the D-Day landings and beyond. They organised sabotage of infrastructure to disrupt German forces.

- By supplying weapons, explosives, and equipment, the SOE enabled the French Resistance to carry out key sabotage and guerilla operations that distracted and disrupted German forces, especially ahead of D-Day. This helped delay German reinforcements from reaching the Normandy invasion area.

- Resistance activities organised by the SOE, such as Operation Jedburgh, coordinated local resistance forces to fight alongside the Allied invasion, facilitating rapid advance through France.

- The SOE fostered and supported the work of the French Resistance, which played a vital role in intelligence-gathering, sabotage, and subversion of the German occupation. This political and military contribution was crucial to the liberation of France.

Research and Further Reading References:

1. Burton, Kristen D. 2020. "Siren of the Resistance: The Artistry and Espionage of Josephine Baker." The National WWII Museum | New Orleans. February 1, 2020. https://www.nationalww2museum.org/war/articles/siren-resistance-artistry-and-espionage-josephine-baker.

2. Haynes, Suyin. 2020. "Inside the Stories of the Most Daring Women Spies of World War II." TIME. October 2, 2020. https://time.com/5892932/a-call-to-spy-real-history/.

3. National Army Museum. 2019. "Special Operations Executive | National Army Museum." Nam.ac.uk. 2019. https://www.nam.ac.uk/explore/SOE.

4. The History Press. 2019. "The History Press | Espionage and the SOE." Thehistorypress.co.uk. 2019. https://www.thehistory-press.co.uk/world-war-ii/espionage-and-the-soe/.

5. "Seven Stories from Special Operations Executive." n.d. Imperial War Museums. https://www.iwm.org.uk/history/seven-stories-from-special-operations-executive.

6. "SOE: The Secret British Organisation of the Second World War." Imperial War Museums. 2023. https://www.iwm.org.uk/history/soe-the-secret-british-organisation-of-the-second-world-war.

7. Mundy, Liza. 2019. "World War II's Female Spies and Their Secrets." The Atlantic. The Atlantic. May 12, 2019. https://www.theatlantic.com/magazine/archive/2019/06/female-spies-world-war-ii/588058/.

8. Imperial War Museums. 2018. "Spies, Saboteurs and D-Day." Imperial War Museums. 2018. https://www.iwm.org.uk/history/spies-saboteurs-and-d-day.

9. Savage, Deborah. 2022. "Women Who Risked Everything: Female Spies of World War II." Www.lapl.org. March 10, 2022. https://www.lapl.org/collections-resources/blogs/lapl/women-who-risked-everything-female-spies-world-war-two.

10. Durn, Sarah. 2022. "The Female Spies Who Helped Win World War II." Atlas Obscura. April 5, 2022. https://www.atlasobscura.com/articles/female-spies-world-war-2.

11. Laurenceau, Marc. 2016. "French Resistance in Normandy - D-Day." D-Day Overlord. 2016. https://www.dday-overlord.com/en/battle-of-normandy/resistance.

12.   Weiss, Steve. 2015. "The Resistance as Part of Anglo-American Planning for the Liberation of Northwestern Europe." Edited by Christian Bougeard and Jacqueline Sainclivier. OpenEdition Books. Rennes: Presses universitaires de Rennes. July 9, 2015. https://books.openedition.org/pur/16351?lang=en.

13.   Foreign and Commonwealth Office, SOE Adviser, Foreign Office, SOE Adviser, Foreign Office, Special Operations Executive, and Ministry of Economic Warfare, Special Operations Executive. 1936. "Records of Special Operations Executive." The National Archives (UK). 1936. https://discovery.nationalarchives.gov.uk/details/r/C153.

XIV

Confronting Collaboration:
Dilemmas and Moral Choices

During the Nazi occupation of France, the resistance encountered a significant challenge - collaboration. This involved individuals or groups aligning themselves with the occupying force actively or passively. Although not unique to World War II, this phenomenon has existed in war and occupation throughout history. However, its political and historiographical understanding has been influenced by the events of the Second World War and its aftermath.

During the occupation of France, people collaborated with the Nazis in various ways. Some aided the Nazis in identifying and apprehending resistance members, while others sought personal gain and protection by cooperating with the enemy. There were many factors that influenced collaboration, including fear of reprisal, economic necessity, ideological differences, or a desire for power or status. These factors could pressure even those initially sympathetic to the resistance cause.

Two main characteristics were prominent. Firstly, the French leaders faced strong incentives to collaborate because Germany had military domination and was willing to punish non-cooperation. It seemed unlikely that French resistance or collaboration would alter the course of the war and the odds of liberation. Secondly, domestic politics played a significant role in French acquiescence. There were significantly more members of the Resistance and acts of railway sabotage in France's left-leaning departments than in its right-leaning ones.

After France's defeat by Germany in 1940, the Vichy government was established and collaborated with Germany. Despite opportunities to continue fighting or defect from the German orbit later on, French elites widely supported this collaboration, while the mass of nationalistic French citizens passively accommodated it. However, as the war dragged on and living conditions in France worsened, public opinion turned against the Vichy government and the occupying German forces. Throughout the occupation, the French Resistance, working mainly in concert with the London-based Free France movement, increased in strength.

Resistance groups were active throughout German-occupied France and made important contributions to the Allied invasion of Normandy in June 1944. Members of the Resistance provided the Allies with intelligence on German defences and carried out acts of sabotage to disrupt the German war effort. Despite the resistance, many French citizens chose collaboration, which was minimised to a great extent after 1945 by Charles de Gaulle and his supporters.

After the war, the pursuit of Nazi collaborators was driven by several motives, including revenge for those murdered, a desire to see those responsible face justice, and a means of ensuring that criminal acts were brought to light and placed on the official record[7]. Many war criminals were judged only in the 1980s, including Paul Touvier, Klaus Barbie, Maurice Papon, and his deputy Jean Leguay[7].

In conclusion, the issue of collaboration during the Nazi occupation of France was complex and multifaceted, involving a range of motivations and responses from different sections of French society. It remains a significant aspect of the history and memory of World War II in France.

Ethical dilemma

For those in the resistance, collaboration posed difficult moral questions. Should collaboration be considered a betrayal, or should there be room for understanding the complexities of individual choices in such challenging circumstances? While collaboration was seen by many as a betrayal of the French spirit and the fight for liberation, it was essential for the resistance to navigate this moral minefield with wisdom and sensitivity.

One must consider the consequences of categorising individuals solely as collaborators, as there were instances where the line blurred. Some individuals collaborated out of fear for their own lives or the lives of their loved ones. They faced the impossible choice of cooperating with the enemy to ensure their survival while secretly harbouring sympathy for the resistance cause. Under the facade of collaboration, they may have provided crucial information to undermine Nazi operations or shielded resistance members from capture. Their collaboration became a camouflage, allowing them to operate from within the enemy's web, multiplying their potential for a positive impact.

Others, despite their collaboration, may have possessed a profound understanding of the resistance's mission and objectives. Deeply aware of the stakes, they engaged in sabotage and subversion, compelled by a dual allegiance. Their actions were rooted in the delicate balance between personal survival and an unwavering commitment to the liberation of their homeland. These individuals exposed themselves to grave risks, using their collaboration as a covert vehicle for providing intelligence, destabilising the Nazis, and saving countless lives.

The resistance, meanwhile, faced the difficult task of distinguishing between the truly repentant collaborators and those whose actions were irredeemable. In some cases, trials were held after the liberation to determine the degrees of collaboration and punish those who had actively harmed the resistance. Yet, even these trials were not without controversy, as some argued that the conditions of occupation had forced ordinary citizens into making impossible choices. The resistance leaders pondered the moral implications of their pursuit of justice, seeking a balance between retribution and compassion. They had to navigate the fine line between holding individuals accountable for their actions and acknowledging the entangled web of fear and circumstance often dominating their choices.

Collaboration also brought the resistance face to face with the issue of forgiveness. Could those who had collaborated during the occupation era be redeemed and reintegrated into society after the liberation? The resistance had to navigate this question, weighing the need for justice against the potential for reconciliation in a divided nation. The challenges of post-war reconstruction and re-establishing a sense of national identity seemed insurmountable at times. Forgiveness required forgiving individual collaborators and addressing the collective guilt and shame that burdened a society haunted by their collaboration. The resistance leaders understood the importance of constructing a narrative that acknowledged the nuance and complexity of collaboration without compromising the values of justice and memory.

As the war concluded and France emerged from the shadows of occupation, the country faced the difficult task of rebuilding and reconciliation. The collective memory of collaboration and the trauma of occupation would leave deep scars on French society. The dilemmas and moral choices faced during this time would continue to resonate, challenging individuals and communities to confront their complicity or resistance in the face of oppression.

Research and Further Reading References:

1.   Kocher, Matthew Adam, Adria K. Lawrence, and Nuno P. Monteiro. 2018. "Nationalism, Collaboration, and Resistance:

France under Nazi Occupation." *International Security* 43 (2): 117–50. https://doi.org/10.1162/isec_a_00329.

2.   Imperial War Museums. 2018. "Spies, Saboteurs and D-Day." Op.Cit.

3.   Lenaburg, Jerry. n.d. "A Book Review by Jerry Lenaburg: Fighters in the Shadows: A New History of the French Resistance." Www.nyjournalofbooks.com. Accessed November 28, 2023. https://www.nyjournalofbooks.com/book-review/fighters-shadows.

4.   Gerwarth, R., & Gildea, R. (2018). Introduction. *Journal of Modern European History.* https://doi.org/10.17104/1611-8944-2018-2-175

5.   Barno, David W. , and Nora Bensahel . 2019. "Powerful Lessons from Spring Break in World War II France." War on the Rocks. April 23, 2019. https://warontherocks.com/2019/04/powerful-lessons-from-spring-break-in-world-war-ii-france/.

6.   Boissoneault, Lorraine. 2017. "Was Vichy France a Puppet Government or a Willing Nazi Collaborator?" Smithsonian. Smithsonian.com. November 9, 2017. https://www.smithsonianmag.com/history/vichy-government-france-world-war-ii-willingly-collaborated-nazis-180967160/.

XV

Liberation: The Impact and Legacy of French Resistance

The moment of liberation in France marked the ultimate success of the French Resistance and signalled the beginning of the end for the Nazi occupiers. The impact of the Resistance on the liberation of France cannot be understated—it was a transformative force that not only weakened the German forces but also served as an inspiration for future struggles for freedom worldwide.

The French Resistance, born out of a fiercely patriotic and determined spirit, operated in various ways using overt and covert methods. Underground networks provided safe houses, communication channels, and logistical support. These networks comprised diverse groups, including fighters from previously organised resistance groups like the Communists and the Gaullists and ordinary citizens who rallied around the cause. They formed a united front against the occupiers, driven by a shared vision of reclaiming their country.

Resistance fighters took on various roles, each contributing to the overall objective of liberating France. Their acts of sabotage on infrastructure and military targets were both disruptive and demoralising to the occupying forces. Targeting key German installations, communication hubs, and supply lines hampered the enemy's ability to sustain their troops and fight effectively. Train lines were sabotaged, strategic bridges destroyed, and ammunition depots rendered useless. These actions often required immense courage and resourcefulness, as sabotage attempts had to be executed quickly and undetected, often under the watchful eyes of the enemy.

In addition to their acts of sabotage, the Resistance focused on gathering vital intelligence. Covert operations were conducted, with resistance members infiltrating German-controlled organisations and even collaborating with double agents. They risked their lives to provide crucial information to the Allies, enabling them to plan their military strategies and optimise their approach as they advanced through France. This intelligence proved mainly instrumental during the planning and execution of the D-Day invasion, as the Resistance provided valuable insights into enemy defences, troop movements, and fortified positions.

As Allied forces advanced through the country, the Resistance fighters joined the frontlines, working hand-in-hand with the liberating armies. Their knowledge of the local terrain, the layout of enemy defences, and the identification of hidden threats proved invaluable to the success of the military campaign. Their presence also provided a much-needed boost in morale for the Allied forces and the French population, as they symbolised the indomitable spirit and determination of the French people.

The liberation of France was not without sacrifice. Many brave Resistance fighters lost their lives in the final push for freedom. Their selfless acts of heroism and unwavering dedication to the cause remain a testament to the human capacity for courage and resilience in the face of adversity. The sacrifice made by these individuals has forever left an indelible mark on the nation's collective memory, with countless memorials and commemorative plaques serving as reminders of the courage and sacrifice of the Resistance fighters.

The French Resistance's impact on France's liberation went beyond the immediate military victory. It served as a source of inspiration and hope for the French, who had endured years of occupation and oppression. The Resistance demonstrated that defiance and resistance were possible and necessary in the face of tyranny. Their actions sparked a renewed sense of courage and unity among the French population, strengthening their resolve to regain their freedom. This resolute spirit infected the occupied territories, inspiring acts of resistance and defiance across the country and disproving the Nazi propaganda that claimed French collaboration and submission.

The legacy of the French Resistance is deeply ingrained in France's collective memory. It reminds the nation of individuals' moral choices during the occupation and the consequences of collaboration with the enemy. The Resistance is a symbol of morally justifiable resistance against tyranny, urging future generations to question authority and defend their liberties. Mayors of towns and cities throughout France continue to honour these brave men and women by renaming streets, squares, and public spaces after them, ensuring their memory lives on in the nation's heart.

Beyond France, the impact and legacy of the French Resistance extend to the global context. It stands as a beacon of hope, demonstrating the power of grassroots movements and the strength of ordinary citizens when united against injustice. The courageous actions of the Resistance fighters have served as inspiration for countless struggles for freedom and human rights around the world. From anti-colonial movements to civil rights movements, their legacy continues to resonate, emphasising the importance of fighting oppression and standing up for justice and equality.

In conclusion, the liberation of France was the culmination of years of resistance, sacrifice, and unwavering bravery. The impact of the French Resistance on the course of history is immeasurable, and its legacy will forever serve as a reminder of the indomitable spirit of the French people. The memory of their struggle and sacrifice will continue to inspire future generations to fight for freedom, justice, and human rights, serving as a testament to the enduring power of resistance and the triumph of the human spirit. The French Resistance exemplifies the strength that can emerge from the darkest times and the transformative impact of collective action in the face of adversity.

The external impact

The impact of the French Resistance during World War II on other national liberation movements can be seen in several ways:

1. Inspiration: The French Resistance inspired other national liberation movements, demonstrating that a determined and organised resistance could challenge and weaken a powerful occupying force. This inspired other movements to fight for their freedom and independence from colonial powers, such as the British and the French.

2. The French Resistance's use of guerrilla warfare, sabotage, and intelligence gathering served as a model for other national liberation movements. Various movements have adopted these tactics in their struggles against colonial powers, such as the wars of national liberation in Asia and Africa or the movement of Islamic Resistance (Hamas) against Israeli occupation of Palestinian territories.

3. International support: The French Resistance's success in gaining international support, particularly from the Allies, highlighted the importance of securing external backing for national liberation movements. Other movements applied this lesson as they sought assistance from foreign powers, such as the Soviet Union, which pledged support for wars of national liberation worldwide.

4. Political impact: The French Resistance's role in the eventual liberation of France demonstrated the potential political impact of national liberation movements. This encouraged other movements to pursue their goals of independence and autonomy, leading to the decolonisation of many territories in Asia and Africa after World War II.

In summary, the French Resistance's impact on other national liberation movements was significant, providing inspiration, tactics, strategies, and lessons on the importance of international support and political impact. These lessons were applied by various movements in their struggles for independence from colonial powers, contributing to the wave of decolonisation that swept across Asia and Africa in the post-World War II era.

Research and Further Reading References:

1. "Strategy - Strategy and Wars of National Liberation." n.d. Encyclopedia Britannica. https://www.britannica.com/topic/strategy-military/Strategy-and-wars-of-national-liberation.
2. Manelli, Gani. "Partisan politics in World War II Albania: the struggle for power, 1939-1944." *East European Quarterly* 40, no. 3 (2006): 333+. *Gale Academic One-File* (accessed November 28, 2023). https://link.gale.com/apps/doc/A153898902/AONE?u=anon~96b4b5c3&sid=googleScholar&xid=a504df7b.
3. "Liberation and Legacy." n.d. The National WWII Museum | New Orleans. https://www.nationalww2museum.org/war/articles/liberation-and-legacy.
4. Office of the Historian. 2019. "Decolonization of Asia and Africa, 1945–1960." State.gov. 2019. https://history.state.gov/milestones/1945-1952/asia-and-africa.
5. Biggio, Jr., Charles P. 1966. "THE USSR and the NATIONAL LIBERATION MOVEMENT." *US Army War College*. https://apps.dtic.mil/sti/pdfs/ADA510154.pdf.

XVI

Lessons from History: Reflections on Freedom and Resistance

The struggle for freedom and resistance against oppression has been a recurring theme throughout history and deeply resonates with the human spirit. An exemplary instance of this fierce fight can be found in the heroic acts of the French Resistance during the dark days of Nazi occupation. As we explore this historical period, we encounter a wealth of profound insights that continue to guide us in our own pursuit of justice and liberty.

At the heart of the French Resistance lay the fundamental principle of unity. In the face of a formidable and remorseless enemy, ordinary individuals from diverse backgrounds set aside their differences and joined forces in a collective endeavour to protect their land and their way of life. Communist resistance groups worked alongside conservative nationalists, and intellectuals collaborated with farmers and factory workers. The unity that emerged from this unlikely alliance demonstrated the power of collective action and the indomitable spirit that arises when a common purpose unites people from all walks of life. This is a great lesson for the Palestinians still struggling for their independence, which they will not achieve divided, but only united.

Resilience and perseverance were the bedrock upon which the French Resistance stood. In the face of overwhelming odds, resistance fighters braved constant surveillance, infiltration, and the ever-present threat of betrayal. They understood that their dedication to the cause and their unwavering belief in the inherent rights of humanity demanded an un-yielding commitment. Their extraordinary resilience served as a beacon of hope in the darkest times, reminding us that the fight for freedom is not meant for the weak-hearted but is a testament to the strength and endurance of the human spirit. This is also true for the Palestinians and any people struggling for freedom from oppression.

Undoubtedly, one of the most remarkable aspects of the French Resistance was its prowess in gathering crucial intelligence and informa-tion. Amidst the shadows of secrecy, resistance fighters became adept at acquiring knowledge of enemy movements, vital strategic plans, and hidden weapon caches. Their clandestine operations involved spies, double agents, and courageous individuals willing to risk everything to obtain vital information. But their role extended beyond gathering in-telligence; it was in their ability to distribute this information that their true power lay effectively. Their networks spread like wildfire, sharing intelligence with the Allies, sabotaging German operations, and disrupt-ing the Nazi war machine. Thus, the French Resistance taught us that knowledge is not only power but a potent weapon against oppressive regimes capable of changing the course of history.

Central to the story of the French Resistance is the powerful asser-tion that the fight for freedom belongs not just to the elite few but to every citizen. Men, women, and even children played vital roles in this titanic struggle, becoming active participants in the pursuit of liberty. They defied occupation forces through acts of sabotage, disseminated underground publications to foster morale, and sheltered Allied sol-diers behind enemy lines. No longer confined by traditional gender roles, women boldly took on dangerous missions, displaying incredible bravery and resourcefulness. Even children, too young to comprehend the full implications of their actions, worked as couriers, delivering messages and supplies under the watchful eyes of wary German patrols. Their courage and determination illustrate that the fight for freedom is not limited by social status or circumstance. It serves as an enduring reminder that the actions of ordinary individuals can transform the course of history.

Ethical dilemmas loomed large within the French Resistance and tested the moral fabric of its members. Faced with unimaginable choices —such as collaborating, betraying fellow fighters under torture, or sacrificing oneself for the sake of others—the resistance fighters demonstrated remarkable moral courage. Even under the most severe duress, they risked their lives to protect their comrades. Their daily decisions while operating in covert networks showcased the power of individual conscience and the resolute belief in the greater good. These ethical choices were not limited to their resistance work but extended to their interactions with their occupied communities. The resistance fighters emphasised compassion and empathy, providing food, shelter, and care to those in need, refusing to let the darkness of occupation extinguish their humanity. The study of their decisions serves as a timeless guide, challenging us to confront the complexities of moral decision-making and to safeguard the principles of justice, even in the direst of times.

In conclusion, the French Resistance remains an indelible chapter in the annals of history, providing profound lessons that resonate with the human spirit. Unity, resilience, knowledge, active citizenry, and moral courage are enduring pillars of the struggle for freedom and resistance against oppression. The legacy of the French Resistance serves as a beacon of hope, reminding us that the collective power of the human spirit, ignited by a shared yearning for justice and liberty, can overcome the darkest of adversities.

XVII

Postscriptum

In the shadow of German occupation and the collaborationist Vichy regime, a brave and determined group of individuals emerged in France during World War II – the French Resistance. This clandestine movement, composed of men and women from diverse backgrounds, played a crucial role in challenging the Nazi occupation and laying the foundation for the liberation of France.

Triggered by the country's swift defeat in 1940 and the subsequent division of France into occupied and Vichy-controlled zones, the Resistance formed as a response to the regime's collaboration with the Germans. Its members, driven by a deep sense of patriotism, sought to oppose the occupiers, restore national sovereignty, and protect the French population, particularly vulnerable groups such as Jews and political dissidents.

The Resistance consisted of various networks and groups, each with its specific focus and methods of operation. These networks spanned the entire country, from major cities like Paris to small towns and rural areas. Two prominent resistance movements were the communist-led Francs-Tireurs et Partisans (FTP) and the noncommunist Mouvements Unis de la Résistance (MUR). However, numerous other groups, networks, and individuals played their part, demonstrating the extent and diversity of the resistance movement.

Sabotage, guerrilla warfare, intelligence gathering, and propaganda became key elements of the Resistance's activities. Acts of sabotage targeted crucial infrastructure such as railroads, communication lines, and factories, disrupting German operations and hindering their war efforts. Resistance members, often operating under code names, risked their lives to obtain and transmit valuable intelligence to the Allies, helping with strategic planning and coordinating military action.

Sabotage operations varied widely, ranging from minor vandalism to large-scale destruction. In some cases, Resistance members targeted German military installations, ammunition depots, and armouries, aiming to hamper the enemy's ability to wage war. They disrupted transportation by derailing trains, destroying tracks, and sabotaging bridges. They also targeted factories producing war materials, limiting the Germans' access to supplies necessary for their military ambitions.

Resistance fighters engaged in guerrilla warfare, ambushing German troops and attacking supply convoys. These hit-and-run tactics inflicted casualties on the enemy and demoralised their forces. Guerrilla actions often required intricate coordination between disparate Resistance groups and careful planning and resourcefulness to avoid detection and capture.

Intelligence gathering was another crucial aspect of Resistance operations. Members infiltrated German-controlled organisations and institutions and collaborator networks to gather information on enemy activities and plans. They risked exposure and certain death to provide Allied forces with strategic insights into German troop movements, fortifications, and potential targets. Wireless radio operators played a particularly vital role, serving as the lifeline between the Resistance and the Allies. Their broadcasts contained encoded messages and reports, enabling coordination and planning on a broader scale.

The Resistance also engaged in subversive propaganda, disseminating leaflets, newspapers, and clandestine radio broadcasts to inspire the French population and challenge German ideology. These publications exposed the crimes of the Nazis, demolished their propaganda, and urged French citizens to resist and persist. The distribution of clandestine newspapers, such as "Combat" and "Libération," maintained the spirit of defiance among the French, fostering unity and strengthening their resolve.

One of the most notable accomplishments of the Resistance was their critical role in gathering intelligence for the D-Day invasion on June 6, 1944. The Resistance provided invaluable information on German troop deployments, fortifications, and coastal defences through its intelligence networks. This information greatly assisted the Allied forces in planning and executing the successful invasion of Normandy, a critical turning point in the war.

The Resistance's activities were not without risks and sacrifices. Resistance members faced constant danger, as their actions were met with brutal retaliation by the Germans and Vichy collaborators. Many were captured, tortured, and executed by the occupying forces. The Germans responded to resistance activity with widespread reprisals, often levelling entire villages and towns, leaving a trail of destruction and loss.

Despite the immense risks, the French Resistance maintained its operations throughout the war, increasing in strength as time passed. As the Allies made their way through France, the Resistance played a crucial role in disrupting German lines of communication, carrying out attacks against retreating German forces, and aiding the advancing Allied armies.

Furthermore, the Resistance played a pivotal role in exposing the atrocities committed by the Nazis. Resistance fighters documented mass killings, executions, and deportations, shedding light on the Holocaust and bringing attention to the crimes against humanity being committed on French soil. Their efforts contributed to international awareness and condemnation of these heinous acts, a significant step towards justice and accountability.

On August 25, 1944, as Allied forces entered Paris, the French Resistance joined the citizens in a momentous uprising against the Germans.

The city, liberated after years of occupation, celebrated both its freedom and the triumph of its brave Resistance fighters.

Fueled by their unwavering determination and love for their country, the French Resistance left an indelible mark on France's history. Their courageous actions and sacrifices remind us of the power of ordinary individuals coming together in the face of tyranny, fighting for freedom and justice, and preserving human dignity. The French Resistance stands as a testament to the strength of the human spirit and the unwavering desire for liberty in the face of adversity.

In the same collection:

The Right to Resist: Zionism and Fascism (Ebook: November 2023).

Other collections:

- Children of Gaza: Requiem For a Civilisation In Decline (Hichem Karoui).
- The Sabotage: How the USA Planned to Undermine China's Belt and Road Project (GEW Reports & Analyses Team).
- Silence Amidst The Storm: Report On the Arab States' Positions Regarding Israeli War In Gaza. (GEW Reports & Analyses Team).
- Oceanic Oases Under Threat: Climate Change and its Toll on Mediterranean, Gulf, and Indian Ocean Enclaves (GEW Reports & Analyses Team).
- Unplugged: Mental Health And Well-being In The Digital Age (GEW Reports & Analyses Team).
- The Next Frontier: The Future of Science and Technology (GEW Reports & Analyses Team).

www.ingramcontent.com/pod-product-compliance
Lightning Source LLC
Chambersburg PA
CBHW072204090426
42740CB00012B/2382